'Keith Hebden is part of a long and rich tradition of radical Christian clergy whose faith and cold anger drive them to act and thereby seek to challenge the principalities and the powers. In his thoughtful new book *Re-enchanting the Activist* he records his actions, the stories of others and the lessons learned on this journey. This story starts with the lone but "enchanted" activist but progresses to the activist as teacher, mentor and team player as the quest – seeing the development of people "in the right relationships" working for justice together. Keith is a great storyteller. His book is full of advice for readers who seek to act not out of anger or hatred but out of love and a deep spirituality. "Re-enchantment", the book argues, comes from following the African proverb – "if you want to go fast – go alone, but if you want to go far – go with others!"'

– *Neil Jameson, Founder*
and Executive Director of Citizens UK

'Keith gets to the heart of what it means to be a true activist. Those dedicated to changing this world, regardless of whether they have a faith or not, will find wisdom here. For all who want to be part of a better world, but have been close to giving up, these distilled thoughts will surely help to re-enchant your faith in activism.'

– *Chris Howson, liberation theologian*
and author of A Just Church

of related interest

The Forgiveness Project
Stories for a Vengeful Age
Marina Cantacuzino
Forewords by Archbishop Emeritus Desmond Tutu
and Alexander McCall Smith
ISBN 978 1 84905 566 6 (hardback)
ISBN 978 1 78592 000 4 (paperback)
eISBN 978 1 78450 006 1

Towards Better Disagreement
Religion and Atheism in Dialogue
Paul Hedges
ISBN 978 1 78592 057 8
eISBN 978 1 78450 316 1

Sceptical Christianity
Exploring Credible Belief
Robert Reiss
ISBN 978 1 78592 062 2
eISBN 978 1 78450 318 5

RE-ENCHANTING
THE
ACTIVIST
Spirituality and Social Change

Keith Hebden

Jessica Kingsley *Publishers*
London and Philadelphia

First published in 2017
by Jessica Kingsley Publishers
73 Collier Street
London N1 9BE, UK
and
400 Market Street, Suite 400
Philadelphia, PA 19106, USA

www.jkp.com

Library of Congress Cataloging in Publication Data
A CIP catalog record for this book is available from the Library of Congress

British Library Cataloguing in Publication Data
A CIP catalogue record for this book is available from the British Library

ISBN 978 1 78592 041 7
eISBN 978 1 78450 295 9

Printed and bound in the United States

Contents

Acknowledgements

No book is an island, and there are too many people who have contributed to this book to name. These are the people who have taught me, challenged me and cared for me over recent years, helping me begin to learn the craft of enchanted activism. A great teacher and companion has been my friend George Gabriel, who quietly offers much of himself for the sake of others. This book is indebted to the honest wisdom of my wife Sophie and my two children, Martha and Bethany. Being married to an experienced editor and proofreader is also a bonus.

There are people who have shared their stories with me or have allowed me to include their stories in this book, and I am grateful to them for it. While writing this book I have also been in counselling. My thanks to Esther for her work with me but also for the amazing work she does every week getting alongside people as they learn to understand and love themselves again. A big thank you to Natalie Watson of Jessica Kingsley Publishers for encouraging me to write this book in the first place and for helping me develop the idea.

This book was written while I came to the end of my time as a parish priest in Mansfield. The people of the churches and communities here have been a great inspiration and teacher to me and have made me incredibly welcome, none more that St Mark's Church in the centre of Mansfield. My biggest thanks go to them.

Introduction

This book is a reflection on one of the reasons activists become disenchanted with what Emma Goldman, atheist anarchist and mother of the feminist movement, used to call 'the cause'. The German theologian and activist Dorothee Soelle made the claim that 'mysticism is resistance' in her seminal book *The Silent Cry: Mysticism and Resistance*. I came across Soelle's assertion at a time when I most needed it. After several years of faith-based activism with no intentional spiritual practice, I was disenchanted. My religion is Christianity, which was both given to me and taken by me. Although there is a decreasing amount of what was given left, it remains the pool at which I most often drink and I cannot imagine why anyone would go anywhere else. But, while many of the illustrations and ideas come from that tradition, I cannot help but be inspired by many others, particularly Buddhism and animism. If you want a defence of a particular religion, then this book will disappoint. This book is for activists of all faiths and of good faith.

Whether you are reading this as an atheist, or theist, or polytheist, I hope you will still find that it speaks to you.

I have always been what people call 'political'. As a child of six or seven I remember arguing with an adult by insisting on language that did not denigrate people with Down's syndrome. At school, my favourite subjects were the arts and social sciences. When I was about 14, I won a prize in Domestic Science, which I was embarrassed to receive, because when asked which celebrity we would invite for dinner and why, I had written about then member of government Edwina Currie, who had dog-whistled a health scare on salmonella poisoning, and said I would cook scrambled eggs for her. My left-wing teacher loved this and gave me first prize. I was also deeply into my faith in a very senses-oriented way. I would speak in tongues and have visions from God, I would attend church because I wanted to, and I loved to pray. Being a bit of an experience junkie, as I got older, I would also love to push the boundaries in other ways too, whether in terms of physical risk, sexual exploration or substance use. What I regret most is the needless sense of shame as I tried to compartmentalize these parts of me in the way the world felt I ought to. Edwina Currie, who we now know was having an affair with the Prime Minister, could probably sympathize, should she ever accept my – still open – invitation.

As a young adult I discovered that I could at least draw together my passions for social justice and my urge to push boundaries in a framework of religious faith. I discovered political theology and Christian anarchism. I met activists who would scale fences, blockade military bases, set up social centres in squatted buildings and challenge the authority of the state through confrontation with the police. Far from being a barrier to activism, my religious upbringing provided me with a useful narrative framework with which I could understand and develop my political action. I was still getting in trouble, just like when I was a kid at school, only now I felt good about it, rather than ashamed. All of this constant pushing outwards of boundaries, my therapist has helped me understand, was at least partly because I did not want to push the boundaries of what medieval mystic Teresa of Avila called 'The Interior Castle'. It may come as no surprise to you that I gradually came unstuck.

When I was ordained as a deacon and then as a priest in the Church of England, I continued my involvement in politics and non-violent direct action: I organized local residents to successfully challenge local government cuts, and I got involved in environmental activism in the neighbourhood and in community development work. All this energized me and was informed by my understanding of Jesus as an organizer and activist with an entirely social task. The more I got involved in community organizing and direct action the less interested I became in any spiritual foundations to what I was doing. While I was still struggling with my new establishment role, I was also experiencing a number of big challenges in my personal life, including the illness and death of my dad. I realized I did not have the internal resources to manage these external pressures: I did not know who I was or have a spirituality that shaped my religious life. It was at this point that I discovered two important mystical authors who were also activists who threw me a lifeline: Simone Weil and Dorothee Soelle. Some of their ideas will be picked up on throughout this book, but that will be just the tip of the iceberg. I encourage you to read them for yourself if you have not done so already.

Of the many stories Soelle tells the one with which I am most familiar is the biblical story of Mary and Martha: sisters who offered hospitality to Jesus in two distinct ways. Martha worked hard to make sure that the physical needs of Jesus and his disciples were met while Mary sat in Jesus' company and enjoyed him. I had identified myself with Martha, the activist, and had forgotten Mary, the mystic. But Soelle contends that what we lack is the balance of the two. She writes that, 'Real contemplation gives rise to just actions; theory and praxis are in an indissoluble connection.' I began to see 'faith' as an experiment in divine engagement whereby any abstract or untestable theology was superfluous. The words of Saint Paul, often quoted at weddings, illustrate the spirit of this approach: he writes, 'If I speak in the tongues of mortals and of angels, but do not have love, I am a noisy gong or a clanging cymbal' (1 Corinthians 13.1). A letter by Jesus' brother James makes the same point: 'Show me your faith without works, and I by my works will show you my faith' (James 1.18).

Burnout and depression seem to be common among activists. Over the years I have discovered that so many of the activists I admire struggle with mental health problems brought about, or exacerbated by, their activist lifestyles. Among environmentalists in particular I have noticed that some activists have become totally disillusioned and embittered by years of what feels like fruitless struggle for change. This book is for them and for anyone who wants to change the world without having a breakdown in the process. Activism should be enlivening and enchanting. Enchantment should animate us to work for a better world. Anything short of these two experiences will only lead to ill health and a lonely rage. And nobody wants that.

In Islam there is a wonderful word *taqwa*. It refers to the constant and continuous awareness of the presence of God. *Taqwa* is not arrived at suddenly or achieved through effort but rather cultivated through mystical practice. I once heard Archbishop Emeritus Rowan Williams say that prayer is not something we get better at but is more like an environment we become more comfortable in. For Williams prayer is largely the act of mystical contemplation. A few years ago, I spent 40 minutes each day attempting stillness. As someone who doesn't instinctively open up to others or connect with the pain and pleasure that other people around me feel I found myself beginning to empathize. I now feel emotions more readily and appropriately, laugh and celebrate more spontaneously. I don't suppose you can measure this, and I don't really want to measure it anyway.

As we develop Soelle's mysticism of resistance further, we learn to feel with all our senses and become fully present to the material and non-material oneness of all things. We must also learn what death and dying mean for our bodies and what it means to live abundantly with death as a connection with the earth. As we become comfortable with breathing, feeling, fasting and dying, we can re-enchant ourselves as activists.

In the Jewish tradition there is a saying from the prophets: 'Do justice, love mercy, and walk humbly with your God' (Micah 6.8). It is sometimes understood that only the 'walk humbly' bit is about God but it would make more sense of the meaning to say, 'Do justice with your God, love mercy with your God and walk humbly with your God.' Religious people of all faiths are often very good at the 'Love mercy' part of this mandate: we can take care of those who are on the sharp end of unjust and broken systems by clothing the naked, feeding the hungry and visiting those who are in prison. This is an important set of activities, but it is not what I mean by 'activism'. Activism is the willingness to ask the question,

'Why?' It is not enough to be steam valves for a system under pressure, allowing the system to continue with a few tweaks of mercy that stop it from blowing up. We must be whistle-blowers against the powers that leave some of us destitute or oppressed. So often we are so busy being steam valves that we feel like we have no time to rail against what is wrong with society. The answer is to place the whistle directly onto the valve and let people loudly blow off their own steam until the cry of marginalized people becomes impossible to ignore. This is activism; as pioneer community organizer Saul Alinsky put it, there is the 'world as it is' and the 'world as it should be', and we need to recognize that we live in the world as it is but not let go of our expectations of the world as it should be.

There are seven chapters to this book, each one taking on a philosophical and spiritual question and giving it a framework of practical mysticism. Though not exhaustive, the practical spiritual exercises are meant to invite the reader into their own exploration of which practices re-enchant you. In Chapter 1, 'Losing Yourself', we will look at what it means to exist and whether existence even holds any meaning. We will look at this deeply important question from the perspectives of politics, science, philosophy and experience and find that there is a vital tension between the ideas of self and non-self. In Chapter 2, 'Reclaiming Yourself', we will discover that the self is only ever partly revealed but is always borne witness to by the earth from which we came. How we choose to express ourselves is a political choice that can nurture and inform our activism. We will explore the mystical practice of contemplative prayer as a means of knowing the oneness of all things rather than simply knowing *about* the oneness of all things. No book can teach mysticism or enchantment, only life can do that.

In Chapter 3, 'Letting God Go', we tackle the concept of divinity head on and find that theism is not always as sure of itself as it so often seems. There are plenty of arguments for theism that, when unpacked carefully, are simply smoke and mirrors and amount to a functional atheism. There are plenty of atheists who, unencumbered with the self-made idols we call 'God', are much more mystical than those of us who call ourselves theists. In the end, Chapter 4, 'Reclaiming God', reminds us that God is not something to be believed in as much as God is something or someone we choose to participate in or with. Having deconstructed ideas of God in order to see how both those who call themselves theists and those who do not can find a spiritual language we will reclaim a God of the gaps who is beyond belief. Here I give examples of public litany to whet your appetite for actions that go beyond protest into the realms of spirituality and the arts as spiritual practice. More importantly, we explore the ethical implications of understanding God and justice relationally rather than in terms of orthodox belief.

In Chapter 5, 'Re-enchanting Religion', we will look at how religion has often been the scapegoat for activist ire despite the self-evident positive impact that religious communities so often make in terms of social reform and cohesion and organized hospitality and care. We will define religion broadly as a community of people who are committed to being spiritual and social agents of change. For some people, religion is found in large-scale institutions, for others it is found around the dining table. We will carefully examine the shadowy side of both religion and belonging to be better equipped to both belong to others and refunction the communities that we belong to, so that they face outwards and seek the common good. Our spiritual practice is community, seeing others as gift and submission as freedom.

In Chapter 6, 'Enchanted by Affliction', we will look at the difficult subject of suffering. But we will look deeper than that to what the French mystic Simone Weil called 'affliction'. When we allow ourselves to own our personal affliction and look for signs of divinity in it, then we may also reach out to the affliction experienced by others either through symbolic action or real practical sacrifice. This is compassion and is the stuff of lament and social change. In this chapter I will give an outline of a particular example of symbolic compassion: fasting in solidarity with others. Compassion is the lifeblood of activism and draws us away from superficial do-gooding and into a more nuanced and respectful understanding of oppression.

In the final chapter, 'Between Heaven and Earth', we look at our attitudes to death and dying and our need to personally reconnect with all nature and its cycles of death and life. Seeing the dynamic animistic reality of all creation we are re-enchanted, even re-wilded, so that we can express the pleasures and pains that nature experiences as witnesses of environmental degradation. Again we will look at spiritual practices that help open the door to a re-enchanted understanding of the earth and how we relate to the 'dust from which we come and to which we will return'.

To be a spiritual person is within easy reach of any one of us. It does not require sainthood or Gandhi-like self-discipline. All it requires is a willingness to experiment faithfully with techniques and habits that form our character and connect us with mystery. There are many tried and tested tools and techniques to pick up and learn from. Mysticism is not only the extreme ecstasies that we might associate with the most famous mystics. We are all beginners when it comes to knowing reality from illusion and our spiritual habits will faithfully form us into mystical creatures. To be enchanted is simply to let compassion connect our mysticism with our practical action. We are enchanted, because we see, lose and find ourselves in the broken world around us and participate with it, conspire with it, for the common good. The purpose of this book is to invite you, the reader, to join in with this experiment: to create spiritual habits that lead to mystical experiences that re-enchant our activism.

1

Losing Yourself

Sometimes breathing feels like drinking. You know when you're really thirsty and a thick cold smoothie hits the back of your throat? Like that. On a holiday in Ireland, I had cycled, alongside my wife Sophie, from Belfast on the north east of Ireland to the north-western coast, covering about 50 miles a day – which for us was plenty – and camping at night. I will never forget the day we arrived after hours riding through driving rain on a remote peninsula only to discover that the youth hostel on our map had been closed for months. We pitched our tent on a grass verge and bedded down, tired and soaked by the heavy downpour. When we woke up the next morning, we found ourselves on the edge of a beach overhung by a clear blue sky. We walked over the sands and just breathed it all in. I found myself wanting to swallow the air, almost greedily. On this coastal edge, the rain-cleared air felt unlike air I normally breathe: it could almost be described as delicious. Breathing – just breathing – became a luxurious gift.

And it is a gift. My dad died some years later from something called 'pulmonary fibrosis' or 'scarring of the lungs'. He was insistent that he was mostly fine, pretty much right to the end of his life. He often said, 'I'm alright, it's just my breathing.' 'Yes, Dad,' I said, 'but breathing is sort of important!' I am a big fan of breathing, for its own sake and even as a pastime. In 2014, I was challenged by a spiritual adviser to spend 20 minutes every day in contemplative stillness. Each day I would sit down in the same seat: back straight, feet flat on the ground, body relaxed but upright, and then I would breathe.

To try to avoid worrying about how much time was left, I set a gentle alarm to go off at the end of the time. For the first few days I didn't really trust the alarm and kept opening my eyes to see if it had failed to go off. It hadn't. I decided to focus my attention very deliberately and carefully on just one part of my breath. I recommend this as a method, since it simplifies the experience and makes it more of an intimate encounter your own body. Behind your nose is a large sinus chamber; like a cave in your head. This ancient cavern is quite roomy, and it connects back to your mouth and to your throat. This chamber is the welcoming lobby of your in-and-out breath. It is where it is first introduced to the inside of your body, before it journeys down into your lungs to be transferred, transformed and united with you. I concentrated all my attention on this bit of the journey:

in through the nose, filling this lobby and out again. Nothing else. I gave no thought to the stages of filling up the lungs (top, middle and bottom) that is often usefully attended to in yoga. Twenty minutes on the arrival of the breath in the body; every day for 40 days.

I soon discovered how difficult it is to still the mind and focus attention on a single thing. It got easier, but I would say that by the end of 40 days I was able to manage about 30 seconds of stillness per 20 minutes of mindfulness. Nonetheless, I'm convinced that like others I discovered new things through this practice: none of these things came from thinking or experiencing in the traditional sense of that word. Rather, the changes came about at another level of being that seemed to gradually wear away the distinction between me and the rest of the universe.

While I sat breathing – expiring – I began to 'breathe with' the rest of the material and spiritual reality. To 'breathe with' is to 'con-spire'. I love the idea that attentive breathing is a way in which the individual might conspire with the rest of creation. Perhaps when we hear the word 'conspiracy', we think of powerful elite businesses and government figures plotting to exploit and oppress us; or terrorist organizations planning an abrupt attack on our sleepy civilization. But these conspiracies are pedestrian compared to contemplation: the conspiracy of attentive breathing. Simply attending to our breathing is the starting point of a journey. This journey explores the mystical reality that both exists as a separate self and at the same time does not exist, because breath both enters us as seemingly separate but also becomes part of us as we breathe. Unless we retrace our steps back to the source of all being, we cannot change anything. This is true because we are not able, nor are we morally permitted, to change something we are not a part of. To try to change a universe that we experience as totally separate from ourselves is to treat it as an object to be acted on rather than a unity to be participated with. This experientially disconnected approach to social justice leads to domination and new, perhaps unintended, injustices, because we do not see ourselves in the other. Unless we relinquish our separation and return our souls to 'the other', we cannot be part of the change.

Perhaps you have tried attentive breathing yourself and, like me, you find it a difficult and frustrating experience. Finding a word or phrase to repeat can often be helpful. For some people the simple word *om* repeated can fix the mind like an anchor. In many Indian traditions this word represents an echo of the foundational sound of creation and so is a perfect word to use when inviting a conspiracy with all of time and space. For others it is the Jesus prayer: 'Lord Jesus Christ, Son of God, have mercy on me a sinner,' or simply a single word like 'love' or 'hope'. For me the word hope is a great one because it reminds me of the French *j'espère*, which in turn sounds a bit like 'conspire'. To conspire with all things visible and invisible is to hope for change. If you use this tool, it's important not to get too hung up on the meaning of the word that you have chosen. The meaning should not be part of your contemplation. If you want to spend 20 minutes repeating the word 'love', don't spend 20 minutes thinking about what 'love' means. Empty the word of all meaning. Just focus on the very word itself. To breathe is to both give and take in equal balance. To find a balance of mutuality and co-dependency with the rest of the natural world is to begin to change the world. If we can recognize this in our most primitive and fundamental act – breathing – we can begin to practise it in the wider of sphere of our acting.

Despite the fact mysticism points us towards the strangeness of reality, the word itself is not very mysterious. It simply refers to the possibility of knowing, at some level, that we are not separate from the rest of being. Mystical experience need not involve visions of other worlds and great ecstasies. It is just that we find ways of blurring the space-time boundaries of our perception enough that we begin to integrate all things both internal and external to ourselves. This has ethical implications. Simone Weil, celebrated twentieth-century mystic, writes about the 'death of the I', the only thing we really have to offer, for what she calls 'annihilation' by God. Weil makes annihilation sound like a good thing; most of the time it does not seem that way to us. We cling to our separation, our discernible being, many of us hope that in some way, even after bodily death the 'I' will continue through legacy or through some notion of an incorruptible and separate soul that is still in some way imprinted with a notion of personality.

The experience of feeling like we are not separate can be elating. It can lead soldiers at war to sacrifice their lives for their fellow fighters with whom they see no separation of life. To experience flow as an artist or musician is to have a mystical experience. My wife plays the oboe and is brilliant at it (she crossed that bit out during proofreading, but I kept it in anyway), but when she is at her most brilliant, she is the least aware of her music-making. That is to say that there is no consciousness of self or oboe, or of the score on the sheet. In the moment when a musician is flowing with the music there is pleasure but not consciously so. This is mysticism. It's flow. It's the collapse of our perception of the silos of me, you, them, and that which is beyond us all, as though they were all separate things. Mysticism is not the belief in oneness. Mysticism is the fleeting experience of oneness that leaves echoes of its ethic in our everyday lives.

The self-less

Breathing is vital and pleasurable, but it is also deeply mystical when attended to. When we breathe in, we take in air made of atoms that are separate from our own, and we infuse them physically into our bodies. When we breathe out, we take something that was part of our bodies and send it out into the universe, where it will become a snail or a cloud or some other thing. To breathe in is to say 'yes' to life and to breathe out is to offer proof that all being is one being. Contemplative, or non-verbal, prayer gives us the space to explore the blurred boundaries between self, self-less, and the other. Focus on the breath is one example of contemplative prayer that some find useful. The self is something that we receive by birth and by nurture but it is also something that we construct by our own will. There is give and take in the making of the self and an enchanted self is one that we are active in the creation of.

We construct our self from genetic material and from the stories we are given and by other people, but we also choose to beg, borrow and discard material to reconstruct our self as we learn who we really are. The self is something built via language, emotion and our experience of our own biology and environment. But what about that biology? Take a closer look, and it as much denies us our self as it affirms it. If I eat a sandwich, at what point does the sandwich cease to be a separate thing from the self? Is it in the mouth, the small intestine, or the large intestine? At some point in the process of eating the boundaries between 'me' and 'it' begin to blur.

At the molecular level the same blurring happens. We are made up entirely of atoms, and we are surrounded entirely with atoms. Roughly 96 per cent of your body is made of oxygen, carbon, hydrogen and nitrogen atoms. But those atoms are mostly empty space. A hydrogen atom, for example, is more than 99 per cent nothingness! These atoms come and go over our lifetimes through cell death and chemical change. It is only our perception that allows us to distinguish the self from a wall that the self is leaning against. If we could put on magic spectacles that allow us to see only at an atomic level, we would struggle to see where the wall began and the person ends. This is brilliantly illustrated in the *Matrix* series of films. In *The Matrix*, human minds occupy a computer program while their bodies are farmed by their robot masters. Those who escape the Matrix are able to peer into it through their own computer, but all they see is endless cascading columns of letters and numbers. Same reality: different perspective.

The sixth-century Greek philosopher, Heraclitus, wrote, 'You never step into the same river twice.' The water constantly flows so that at any given moment it is different water, a different shape and dynamic carrying a different load. As the river flows, the bed of the river is lifted, crafted and deposited. We, like rivers, are in constant flux: both on the physical surface and in the depth of our self. The self who woke up this morning is a partial stranger to the self who goes to bed tonight.

You are almost nothing and the little that you are is in constant flow with the little that everything else is.

Even if we scale up slightly from the atom it is hard to tell who is self and who is not. According to celebrated microbiologist Giulia Enders, our guts contain two kilograms of bacteria – 100 trillion of them. At the moment before birth, we are 100 per cent made up of our own cells. By the time we are fully developed, 90 per cent of our mass is made up of bacteria. These bacteria inform how we feel, what sort of foods we can digest, and how our minds respond alongside an intestinal nervous system as complex as the brain of cat, that communicates itself to the conscious mind at the top of our spines in ways that we don't control or understand. We are used to thinking of the unconscious and the conscious mind but in reality we have three unconscious minds: the one in the brain, the one in our guts, and the one that connects those two. So when the philosopher René Descartes wrote those famous words, 'I think therefore I am,' he was just playing around the edges of both being and thinking in a way which we now know, at a biological level, is considerably more complicated and mysterious than we realized.

There is nothing new under the sun, of course. The observation that we are both real and illusion goes back to Buddhism and beyond to the religions of the Indus and beyond even that, perhaps. For Buddhists and modern Hindus, all perceived reality is *maya*, which can be translated as 'illusion'. My favourite story about this is the one about a guru who often irritated a king by going on about the fact that everything was an illusion. One day the king arranged things so that when the guru arrived in the palace grounds, a bull elephant was released to chase him away. The guru ran off, of course, and escaped to the safety of a large tree. The king mocked the wise guru: 'It seems you don't believe your own philosophy, since you ran away from the elephant!' But the guru was quick to reply, 'Ah yes, your highness, but my running away is also an illusion!' Within Buddhist philosophy there is the assertion that we can experience our absence of self as legitimately as we experience being our self. This takes us full circle to contemplation and the importance of emptying our consciousness of our self into the simple act of breathing in and out.

Last summer, I taught my daughters how to skim stones across the surface of a lake. One of the great things about parenthood is that sometimes, even when you're rubbish at something, your children still think you are amazing at it. This was one of those times. The ability to make a stone gently touch the water several times as it travels skipping over the top of the water was a magic trick. Strictly speaking, if you throw a stone into a lake, it should sink immediately. That had been their experience, anyway. Stones touch the water and immediately it enfolds them and draws them down as they disappear below. But to find a flat, round stone and curl it around your finger so that, when released, it manages to only have a nodding acquaintance with the deep lake before it eventually sinks or lands on the other side, is almost a rite of passage. This is a picture of the relationship between our awareness and its subject: the self. We are unable to disappear into the divine and completely lose our sense of self. If we did so we would be no use to anyone, anyway. But if we can learn to maintain some magical defiance of the gravity of the delusion of self we can still greet the non-self often without going under. Because the self, or the illusion that we exist, is not our enemy. In fact, it is vital to our ability to function in a world full of egos: of illusions of self with which we interact. And if neither self nor non-self exist then we can hardly make a hierarchy of them. We learn to skim along the fragile surface of unity with all things. This is what British mystic Evelyn Underhill called 'practical mysticism'. An enchanted activist nurtures a practical mysticism of resistance.

It is not enough for us to understand biologically, politically, psychologically and sociologically that the self is something built to allow us to function when we are out walking the dog and meeting other human beings out walking theirs. We most often experience the absence of self through mystical encounter with the oneness of all things. Spirituality, the awareness of a non-material reality, is a step towards mysticism but it is not the same. To be spiritual is to be awakened to mystery and otherness but to experience mysticism is to be awakened to mystery and oneness. To allow our spirituality and mysticism to transform our relationship with the other is to be enchanted by all that appears separate from us in everyday life. Spirituality should lead to mystical encounter and mystical encounter should lead to enchantment which is, perhaps, our romantic re-engagement with the world. An activist who does not have a mystical life is like a bear who sets traps for itself in the woods. Vanity, powerlessness, despair and machismo all lie in wait for the disenchanted activist. Vanity becomes a trap when we become anxious about whether we exist or not and look beyond ourselves for affirmation of that existence.

2

Reclaiming Yourself

Recently I took the funeral of a wonderful woman who had a difficult ending but a long and happy life with the man she loved. I met him at their home on a sunny spring morning. He wore a three-piece suit and tie, as he always did, and talked about the adventures that he and his wife shared, her friends and hobbies, and disagreements about her end-of-life care. But what struck me most deeply was the way he talked about their long country walks together. 'We would walk for hours without saying a word,' he told me. Giving the funeral address, two weeks later, I reflected that it is in the shared silences that we learn the most about each other. A mourner, in his eighties, whose wife of over 50 years now struggled with dementia, nodded and beamed at me. It is perhaps not impossible to reveal yourself to another; one silent moment at a time. But being yourself and revealing yourself is far from a straightforward task.

'Just be yourself,' I was told, when about to go on a three-day interview. Be yourself? Which one? The well-meant advice is pretty superficial. Which self should I be? Presumably not the one who sits around all day in his dressing gown and boxer shorts eating Pot Noodle sandwiches and watching daytime TV. I have been at least three different versions of myself before breakfast; each human interaction is a new self. If you've ever seen a picture of two masks, a happy one and a sad one, to denote a theatre you might know that this comes from the ancient Greek style of theatre where actors used masks so that the audience knew which character they were currently playing. The Greek word used for this type of mask is *persona*. We usually only connect with people by way of symbolic communication using the various masks in order to convey something of who we are. The wearer of the mask only sees the inside of it: this is what they think they are showing. The other person only sees the outside of the mask. Neither actor sees the real face of the other. The outside of our mask, the person we present, is what other people see. While there is some continuity between what we choose to present and what other people receive they are not entirely the same thing. Most of the time we communicate person-to-person, not self-to-self. Professor Homi K. Bhabha calls this the 'third space', a margin of translation between what we choose to present and what others actually experience.

We arrive with much of our attitudes, habits and interactions predetermined by our genes and by our ancestral heritage. There is a famous icon of the Buddha, as he became enlightened, in which he is sat cross-legged with one palm upright on his lap while the other gently touches the earth. In the story behind this serene image, the demons, led by Mudra, are surrounding and accusing the young prince (who is now the Buddha). They claim that he is not enlightened at all and ask him to produce a single witness. It is at this point that he simply lets one hand fall and touch the earth. The earth immediately responds, 'I bear witness!', and the demons flee. The story is a powerful illustration that we do not simply sit on a mute planet but on thousands of years of history located in places and stories that we do not know, but, from the moment of our birth, they tell us who our community is. Spiritual activist Alastair McIntosh[1] reminds us of the psychodynamic assertion that our self rests on incrementally subconscious but potent layers of family, community, nation, ethnic group, primitive ancestors, animal ancestors and even a 'central life energy' that every expression of selfhood is a fragment of. We arrive at birth with this as a gift and a challenge.

Our self is shaped by our heritage and by those whose desires we mimic. But it is also shaped by the stories told about us. Growing up in our family we, like many other households, had favourite stories we would rehearse. On my first day at nursery school aged three (and a half), I refused to let go of my mum's neck. I clung like a screaming, bawling and deranged orangutan and not even the offer of sweets would pacify me. Once the teacher finally managed to prise me away and reassure my mum I would be fine, I had a great morning. When she came to pick me up later, I was holding hands with Samantha – my first love – smiling away like nothing had happened. A year later my brother arrived at the same classroom, and he too began to cry and experience separation anxiety. Again our mum tried the old, 'When I come and get you, I'll bring you a bag of sweets.' However, this time it worked: he stopped crying instantly and went in. I have no idea how many times our family has retold this story and laughed at all three of us. The lessons were never drawn out but internalized nonetheless. They were intended as illustrations of our personalities. The story that was rarely told happened six months before I started nursery school, and, despite not being quite three years old, I remember it vividly. It was an operation carried out on the orders of a well-meaning but misguided doctor. This was my first memory of being separated from my mum and was so frightening I vividly remember it to this day. If we had not told the story of my first day at school, perhaps I would not have followed the thread back to that awful day in the hospital, but thankfully I have done and, through the support of a good counsellor, I have learnt how to integrate that story into myself too. But it is not just the stories we hear and repeat about ourselves that lend us our sense of self. I often meet families who talk about themselves collectively: 'We've always been a bit psychic in our family,' for example, or 'Her mother was a bit anxious, and so was her aunty.' We convince ourselves that 'The apple never falls far from the tree.'

Philosopher René Girard (1923–2015)[2] claimed that we are shaped by the desires of others, in that we see what they desire: from the very earliest weeks of life we mimic those desires. The urge to copy desire stays with us all our lives and allows others to lead our behaviour. It causes conflict with those we admire the most and those with whom we compete most passionately for a common desired object, status or outcome. An enchanted activist must be constantly aware of the power of this mimetic desire, how it can scupper our attempts at unity but also how it can unite peer groups through a shared desire for a just outcome.

A few years ago, I fasted for 40 days. Two women I know, independently of each other, invited me to interview them about the connection between their self and their relationship to food and the body. I listened and recorded the conversations not knowing what might be learned. Their stories tell us a lot about how our identity is both given and taken. I'll call them Rachel and Alice. Below is some of what they told me. Both women are activists with a religious and spiritual foundation to their political engagement with the world as it is. They are enchanted activists, and so they are also enchanting and world-changing storytellers. Both stories carry a trigger warning: they refer (without describing it) to sexual abuse. You may decide that it's not a good idea for you to read these stories.

Rachel is a peace activist and a member of Overeaters Anonymous. As a child Rachel was repeatedly sexually abused by a friend of her family. She also experienced another form of abuse: early authority figures talked down to her and nurtured an unhealthy relationship with food. Below, she bravely relates her experience, as a young teenager, responding to her abuse.

> I ate masses that evening; masses and masses and masses. I felt ill all the time. And I then decided I wanted to die. So I took every tablet in the house. My mum was hysterical, as she often was anyway. They took me to hospital and put me on a bed and shoved a tube down my throat, and they filled it with water, and they talked about what they did last Saturday night, and I vomited everywhere, and they talked about how happy they were and how happy their life was and how sick the other people in the hospital was and how I was wasting their time and how I was taking up a bed.
>
> And I came home, and I just thought, 'Oh fuck it. It don't matter anyway: he's got twins, he's living somewhere else.' I was very confused. But in the midst of all this; because I had that addiction to food as an emotional thing. You also have the normal stuff with food of: you have a family dinner so my family over eats regularly anyway. So for me to eat similar portions they just go, 'Oh! Family! Big Family! Get it down you; you be alright. Eat your dinner; make sure you clear your plate.' My grandmother always said that if she walked past a chip

shop, she put five pound on. She didn't have to consume any; naturally big. So I lost seven stone, and the only way I could do that was losing weight became my full-time occupation.

[When I'm thin] I feel very, very vulnerable. Because somebody can kneel on my shoulder blades and make me not move. And I'm so confident in my skin that even at my biggest I was a nude model at the polytechnic for the art class, and I did that for a year and a half. My grandmother and my mother were large and powerful women. So it wasn't something to be ashamed of. The only problem I have is that, the shame I have, is that they didn't realize that something else was going on as well.

Alice is also a person with a commitment to her faith community, to spirituality and to social justice. Another enchanted activist. She talks of her experience of being 'conventionally attractive' and how that made her feel obliged to take an identity as sexually available or alluring while appearing intellectually unthreatening to other people.

I was always conventionally attractive and naturally slim and naturally tall, so that I think, you become bound by that in some way, because people have certain expectations of you and those expectations are often low. I was always picked to model things, and I was always picked for photographs and stuff. Girls have never liked me. I've never had girlfriends, because there was always competition, so I joined this new group of friends, really in [the nearby town] this group of punks and 'yobbos' [laughs], dole-ites, students as well; this 'alternative' group of people anyway. And the men went, 'Woohoo! We love her!' And the girls all hated me and I'm actually really nice!

Once I got beat up on the dance floor in Harvey's just because I was there, I didn't do anything; I was never unkind to anyone. I was never, ever, unkind. I wasn't horrible, at all. In fact I was intimidated by most of the women. The older women were fine but the younger ones were dreadful.

I behaved in the way that I thought I should behave based on the way people treated me. I can remember even as a child looking in the mirror and saying, 'I think I'm pretty enough to get married.' So even then there was that social convention that said, 'You need to behave in a certain way.' And I even used to say that my ambition was to marry a rich man and I don't think it ever really was, but it seemed like that was the only thing.

I found my identity in short-term relationships – if you can call them relationships – and I found that that kind of behaviour becomes very needy and its almost addictive, because you meet someone and they come on to you, and you've got low self-esteem, and you don't feel very attractive or you feel that you need to be told you're attractive because that's where you find your worth. So then you're told you're attractive, and then you put out, because that's what you think you have to do. Because they've been nice to me, so I'll be nice to them. And that's how it works. And after all, you know, I'm a girl, and this is what's expected of me.

Alice's experience led to an ongoing struggle with food but in a very different way to Rachel. For Alice, above-normal levels of anxiety led to a cessation of eating altogether for days on end, often without realizing it. Two women – one fighting overeating the other fighting undereating, both learning to survive the self given to them by other people. Both powerfully use the sharing of their stories to help them survive the stories told by others and to reclaim the self. Both women are incredibly inspirational to me: I recall some of my own stories as a man, who could easily have been a peer or sibling of either in generational terms.

 Enchantment through storytelling is contagious and co-transformative. An activist who doesn't tell their own story will quickly become disenchanted and will cease to hear other people's stories, because there is an exchange in storytelling. At a simple level I learned this with my children. When I pick my girls up from school, I want to know about their day. I have learned that if I ask them, 'What did you do today at school?' they will invariably reply, 'Nothing.' Or, at best, they'll tell me what they had for lunch. But, if I say, 'I had a really difficult conversation today and felt sad, but I really enjoyed having a coffee with Vanessa, who has found somewhere to live. What did you do today?' I will get a different answer. The same is true with adults: if we want to lead people into action, we must lead them into a meaningful public relationship with others. This means modelling an appropriate amount of challenge and vulnerability.

We are also given our self when we are told about other people. The adults who raise us will tell us approving and disapproving stories about other people's behaviour. In doing so they give us another layer to our moral and ethical self. We don't want to be subject to gossip and judgement, so we internalize a fear of behaviour that would lead to it. We are given, by others, what we can do, how to feel, and how to behave, according to the degree we receive or reject it. But we can expand this even further.

In the UK at the moment the government is trying to give us our self by making schools teach something they are calling 'British values'. This says a lot about how governments can be both creepy and incompetent. After all, we are not actually shaped by taught values but by shared stories. Stories about Remembrance Day, history lessons, the 1966 World Cup, the 'Winter of Discontent', when striking peaked in the UK before huge reforms against the rights of unions. All these stories give us our self. Where the state is creepy but competent is in the retelling of national stories. Many of these stories are repeated every year; others are ritually repeated irregularly. They are 'British stories', and they are not the same as the events that actually happened. There is no such thing as an objective account of events, only the selective framing of a remembrance. Mostly these stories disenchant us: they make us less socially competent, less emotionally literate and less spiritually aware. To be re-enchanted by stories we must learn how to playfully experiment with them in ourselves and in the telling by and with others. We must choose our stories and learn how to tell other stories of self and nation to challenge the status quo.

The reclaimed self

What about the self that chooses? The reclaimed self is that which we inherit or that forces itself on us. The act of giving someone their sense of self is morally neutral but the act of passively and unquestioningly taking what is given is not. We might be grateful or critical of the given self, but we should never be passive. We must take our self and experiment with what it means to be 'me'. There is now a long tradition of what is often called 'identity politics'. Often this involves marginal communities in the proactive reclaiming of slurs like 'gay', 'queer', 'black' and so on. For others it's the positive assertion of an alternative: 'intersexual' rather than 'androgynous', for example.

I have been fortunate to make several visits to India over the past 20 years. There I met people previously known as 'outcaste' or 'untouchable'. For many former untouchables the term 'Dalit' is now preferred as a way of giving expression to their identity. Early use of the word Dalit dates back to the nineteenth-century social reformer and activist Jyotirao Phule, but it was popularized in the 1970s by the Dalit Panthers, a social justice cultural and literary movement for the liberation of Dalit peoples. The word has several emotive meanings: it can mean 'of the earth', but it is more often translated as 'crushed', 'broken' or 'oppressed'. It might seem odd that hundreds of thousands of communities would choose such a negative self-descriptor, but its proud ownership is a constant act of defiance. They have rejected their given self and taken a self of active resistance to caste prejudice. It was under the leadership of Bhimrao Ambedkar that the new sense of self as Dalit really swept the political scene, as Ambedkar coupled it with a mass movement of conversion to Buddhism (although many Dalits are Hindu, Muslim, Christian or another faith) and to a political vision of state socialism. Ambedkar recognized the powerful role of spiritual renewal as a vital force in taking back the self from an exploitative system.

Often the reclamation of selfhood for one is in tension with the self-reclamation process of another. For example, the womanist movement, in which oppressed black women express the double injustice of prejudice against black people and against women is a challenge to Western feminism. Proponents of womanism have tended to see feminism as privileged and lacking real solidarity. If a white woman is freed from male-privileging domestic servitude because she employs a black woman to cook, clean and look after their children, then this is a narrow feminism indeed. A general response to this since the early 1990s calls on society to recognize that different types of discrimination intersect with one another. We should always be looking out for and speaking of these intersections of discrimination as people navigate the give and take of being yourself.

If you have ever seen the Harry Potter films, you will know that one of the stars of the show, Hermione Grainger, is white. But in the book her ethnicity is never stated. Few people bat an eyelid, since any unstated ethnicity is always white. Until this is challenged, no amount of taking of self-identity can stop those who have been pushed to the margins from being considered as 'abnormal', when whiteness is always the default. We are given role and status, or lack of status, by others or we claim them for ourselves. In the case of the fictional Hermione Granger, the author, J.K. Rowling, has responded positively to challenges[3] to black invisibility in the franchise: 'brown eyes, frizzy hair and very clever. White skin was never specified. Rowling loves black Hermione.'[4] All this identity-taking means those on the margins always have to define themselves, while those who occupy the 'normal' ground have the privileged selfhood in the first place. A straight, white man rarely has to call himself that, he is simply 'a person'. One response to this, in gender terms, has been the word 'cisgender', often shortened to 'cis', which is the antonym to transgender. This is a challenge from transsexual people for cisgender people to take a specific position relative to transgender, or genderqueer, people instead of asserting themselves as a benchmark of normality.

Laurie Penny is a genderqueer feminist writer and an activist. She has been in the public eye for several years as a journalist and feminist but came out as genderqueer in 2015. Below is an edited version of her story published on BuzzFeed.[5]

> I've never felt quite like a woman, but I've never wanted to be a man, either. For as long as I can remember, I've wanted to be something in between. To quote Ruby Rose: I called myself a girl, but only because my options were limited. I always assumed that everyone felt that way.
>
> I was anorexic for large parts of my childhood and for many complex, painful, altogether common reasons, of which gender dysphoria was just one. I felt trapped by the femaleness of my body, by my growing breasts and curves. Not eating made my periods stop. It made my breasts disappear. On the downside, it also turned me into a manic, suicidal mess, forced me to drop out of school, and traumatized my entire family. At 17, I wound up in the hospital, in an acute eating disorders ward, where I stayed for six months.
>
> Psychiatric orthodoxy tends to lag behind social norms, and doctors are very busy people. So it's not their fault that, less than 20 years after homosexuality was removed from the official list of mental disorders, the doctors treating me took one look at my short hair and baggy clothes and feminist posters and decided that I was

a repressed homosexual and coming out as gay would magically make me start eating again.

For five years, I struggled to recover. I tried hard to be a good girl. I tried to stick to the dresses, the makeup, the not being quite so strange and cross and curious all the time. For five years, I shoved my queerness deep, deep down into a private, frightened place where it only emerged in exceptional circumstances.

I regret that there wasn't more language, dialogue, and support for trans and genderqueer kids when I was a teenager and needed it most. I regret that by the time I had found that community and that language, I regret the fear that kept me from coming out for so many years.

The journey I took as I came to terms with my own identity – the journey that will continue as long as I live – all of that has led me to where I am now.

For Penny, not being able to meet the usual expectations of the given self led to many years of building an identity that made sense of their (preferred pronoun) being. Doing so is good for her wellbeing and deeply informs their future as an activist now far less likely to burn out. They (preferred pronoun) have become enchanted with their self and so with others.

Around about the same time as Penny's coming out as genderqueer, another writer and activist took the same courageous public step. Jack Monroe came to public attention as a blogger who, out of personal necessity, was discovering how to cook on a very tight budget as a single parent. In the process they became a prominent anti-poverty campaigner and activist. We worked together, briefly, on the End Hunger Fast campaign in 2014, when thousands of people across the UK fasted in solidarity with those who go hungry in Britain. On cookingonabootstrap.com[6] Monroe tells the story of coming out as genderqueer or transgender.

> It was National Coming Out day, I was on my way home from a 1,000 mile round trip from Southend to Glasgow via Manchester and back again to talk about austerity at Scottish Green Party Conference, and I was tired of my closet full of Underworks binders [clothing for flattening the chest] and denial. I typed the words, saved the tweet as a draft, and tried to call my Dad. He didn't answer, so I texted him instead before I lost my nerve. 'How are things?' he asked. 'Ok. I'm about to come out as transgender. I hope we can talk about it some time.' He replied three minutes later, three minutes I'm not ashamed to admit I spent gripping my phone so hard that the small crack in the screen now splits from top to bottom. 'Of course you can talk to me. It matters not one jot how you express yourself. Unless you become a Tory. Then you can fuck off :)'
>
> I breathed out, reassured him via Aneurin Bevan that 'no amount of cajolery, no attempt at ethical or social seduction' would make me join the Conservative Party, and came out to the world with the prod of a finger.

The increasingly fluid nature of both gender and sexuality in contemporary Western society shocks and frightens many people. Among feminists it has become a hot button topic, dividing people and destabilizing the whole project of deconstructing patriarchy. The biggest challenge, brought about by the courage of people who come out as genderqueer, is whether feminism is primarily about equal rights for women or about bringing patriarchy to an end. For me it's about the latter. People coming out as genderqueer, far from betraying feminist activism, takes us a step closer to realizing a world where womanhood is not equated with proscriptions of any kind. Recently I took my two young daughters shopping, and both of them complained grumpily that there was a blue section for boys and a pink section for girls (yes, this anger is part of their give-and-take identity). At ages six and eight, they are perfectly capable of seeing patriarchal capitalism at work telling them what girls can and cannot buy and where. Would genderqueering of society make them more or less free? More, of course.

In postcolonial studies there has long been a wariness of the idea that if we could only see we are all the same then there will be peace in the world. But when straight white middle-class liberals like me say, 'Basically we're all the same,' we're in danger of assuming that 'the same' is 'like me', which is just another form of monopolizing culture. The alternative can be equally oppressive, the othering of what is called 'Orientalism', when we talk about people different from ourselves in romantic, exotic or quaint terms. For example, when Western 'experts' talk about the Taliban as being 'from the

Middle Ages', they make them an exotic other and fail to see Daesh (ISIS) as a modern response to a modern political context. Both universalizing and generalizing people denies the complexity of oppression and will not lead to lasting social good.

If all this sounds more complicated than enchanting should sound, then take another breath and relax. To fully understand everyone else's politics of self is not the goal. To appreciate the ever-shifting varieties of self-understanding without judgement is the purpose of this mental exercise. If I see a tree heavy with a hundred varieties of fruit, I can either worry about how confusing it is, or I can enjoy what I see and taste. Let the many layers, intersections and tensions of giving and taking selfhood be enchanting. Actively re-enchant your own communities with the joy of self-discovery.

However, we will have to consider self-abandonment too. Or as Nagarjuna, a founder of the Mahayana Buddhist tradition, puts it:

> *There is the teaching of Self*
> *And there is the teaching of not-Self.*
> *But by the Buddhas neither Self nor not-Self*
> *Has been taught as something that exists.*[7]

The enchanted self

I have claimed that we need to hold on to both the self and the self-less in some sort of tension. Just like a stone skimming across the surface of a pond or river so our attachment to self must be light-touch, or we will sink into it and sink also into disenchantment. A well-maintained tension between self and self-less is expressed in a strong ego. Activists, unashamedly, need a strong sense of self.

The ego is found in Moses' mysterious encounter with the Hebrew God in the Jewish tradition. In this story Moses, having fled Egypt, partly in confusion about his own identity, has a mystical experience of the divine in the desert. He has a vision of a bush covered in flames but that does not burn and out of which a voice speaks. The story tells us that Moses was born a Hebrew slave but was brought up in the Egyptian royal household. As an adult he has to navigate these two conflicting identities and decide where his loyalty lies. In the process he kills an Egyptian slave driver, but the act leads not to acceptance by the slaves but a rejection by both communities. During his new life in the desert he is confronted by the ego of God. God has a massive ego.

> But Moses said to God, 'If I come to the Israelites and say to them, "The God of your ancestors has sent me to you", and they ask me, "What is his name?" what shall I say to them?' God said to Moses, 'I AM WHO I AM.' He said further, 'Thus you shall say to the Israelites, "I AM has sent me to you."' (Exodus 3.13–14)

For someone whose identity is in such turmoil, it must have been incredibly intimidating to be confronted by the confidently deconstructed ego of God. God did not need fancy titles or letters after their name; 'I am who I am' is sufficiently great. Of course, a burning bush and a disembodied voice are also quite impressive. It is no coincidence that the Jesus of John's Gospel uses the same formula to equally devastating effect. At the moment of his arrest for insurrection in Gethsemane, on the outskirts of the city of Jerusalem, Jesus and his followers are confronted by soldiers and state officials who demanded that he identify himself.

> Then Jesus, knowing all that was to happen to him, came forward and asked them, 'For whom are you looking?' They answered, 'Jesus of Nazareth.' Jesus replied, 'I am he.' Judas, who betrayed him, was standing with them. When Jesus said to them, 'I am he,' they stepped back and fell to the ground. (John 18.5–6)

Although Jesus spoke Aramaic, the stories of his life were written in Greek. John has Jesus saying 'I am' in Greek, which would normally have been written as 'ego', but John underlines it by having Jesus say *Ego eimi*. This is not a natural way of speaking but could be translated as 'I am I am'. It was the power of John's self-understanding that gave him his authority to act and speak as he did. He was an enchanted activist and did not resort to violence or to running away but stood his ground with confidence. John's take on Jesus knew that the self was both nothing and something and so declared the 'I am' to point both beyond himself, but also to assert authority as a human being with dignity and purpose.

For the past few years I've been very involved in a national non-profit called Citizens UK which is affiliated to the Industrial Areas Foundation (IAF) in the USA. Both of these alliances work to develop leaders and community organizers to have a strong ego and to act with others to bring about a common good. I want to draw a distinction here between ego and selfishness or narcissism (the desire for self-affirming attention). We've all behaved in ways that are selfish from time to time. I've met some powerful leaders who others would say are egotists because they name-drop or love being seen with the right people or nurture a self-consciously flattering self-image. In fact these people have weak egos and are shoring up their insecurities with carefully tailored external projections of self. They often bully others when they feel threatened. By contrast, when we develop a strong ego, we are able either to be prominent and outspoken or to quietly organize in the background. We do whichever is useful and take a position when it's useful and lay it down when it's not. We understand the limits of our self and we value joining with others.

In the small town of Mansfield I have seen head teachers and faith leaders politely but firmly take on local and regional politicians. I've seen young children and formerly homeless adults do the same. They stand up, tell their story and insist on mutuality and a response from those who have power over their lives. When we hold a negotiation with people who have power over us we always begin by credentialling ourselves. We tell the people we are negotiating with who we are and why that should matter to them (usually in terms of the number of people we lead). This is ego. Ego gives us the power to act, which is what activists who want to build the world as it should be all seek.

We develop our own ego and nurture the egos of other people by sharing stories. We choose stories about ourselves, honest, public narratives, which explain who we think we are. These stories tell others who our most important relationships are with, where we put our time, energy and money, who we think we belong to and what our hopes and fears are. If we build a habit of telling selected stories, then inviting listeners to make an exchange, we will begin to learn better how to act together on our shared interests. On an average working week I try to have at least eight one-to-one conversations of this kind, each lasting around 40 minutes. As I do so, I both practise and scrutinize my own stories, and I accept as a gift the stories that others choose to tell. We become credible witnesses to the world as it is and the world as it should be, when we learn to explain who we are in relation to those two worlds. We cannot do so if we are so uncertain of the validity of our witness that we cannot speak or listen to them.

Maggie Kuhn was an activist in the USA who founded the Grey Panthers, a civil rights group that championed the rights of people in nursing homes and challenged prejudice against older people. She was old and had a strong enough ego to know that being old does not mean you do not matter. A quote, now a popular meme for bumper stickers and t-shirts, often attributed to Kuhn, states simply, 'Speak the truth, even if your voice shakes.' In this wonderful call to speak boldly we see that, as we are trying to develop a strong ego, it is equally important to know the limits of our ego but to push past them anyway. If I am too vain to speak out on an issue of injustice because I am afraid that I will falter, this is a fear of what other people will think of me. I should speak out anyway. I should speak out because other people thinking ill or well of me is less important than bringing about the change needed. Like many activists, I have learned this the hard way. I have been called arrogant, racist, the devil, a hypocrite, scum and worse – some of this online, some of it behind my back, and much of it which I will never hear about, thankfully. Perhaps you have been on the receiving end of the same and worse. It is not possible to go on for years as an activist without an ego that can warmly welcome compliments but not be ruled by them and to find gifts in our enemies' words without letting the wounds become permanent scars.

The self is a fragile and illusory thing: it both exists and is nothing. But it is all the more beautiful for that. Children know this experience in their spontaneous joy with blowing bubbles and chasing them until they pop. A bubble is no more than a structure that becomes invisible as soon as the structure is collapsed. It is a boundary between two nothings: the air inside and the air outside of the bubble. It is why it is important that we activists learn to breathe and simply be and not be: to be mystical in our experience of the self and to constantly interrogate the self as it is given, received, reclaimed and rejected. To both lose and discover one's self in action is to be an enchanted activist. With its constant practice, we can and do act in the world as it is to create the world as it should be.

3

Letting God Go

A sociologist arrived in Belfast to run a survey on the religious and political beliefs of residents in an area of historic and ongoing conflict and reconciliation. She was challenged by a subject of her research who turned the questioning back on her, wanting to know if she was a Protestant or a Catholic. 'I'm an atheist,' replied the sociologist, giving herself impeccable neutrality, to which her subject responded, 'Sure you're an atheist, but is it the Protestant or the Catholic God in which you don't believe?' This street-philosopher was making an important point. Atheism is not at all straightforward and is every bit as complex as theism – the belief in a god. But more complex still is the ability to hold in tension the two truths that God both is and is not real. As Simone Weil playfully put it, in one of her notes, 'God exists, God does not exist, where is the problem?' As we shall see, when we worry too much about whether or what God is, we lose the point, which is to participate in God rather than believe. In order to reclaim our participation with the divine we must let go of God, or at least, we must let go of all of our conceptions of God. Each one is an idol.

We have discovered that it is possible and enchanting to take apart our understanding of self and to use contemplative practices to experience the destruction of self. We have also found that in doing so we are free to explore the give and take of the self that we are and to tell the stories that shape us, inviting others to do the same. If it is possible to say that the self is both real and not real, then it is also true of God. God is both real and not real. Or rather, God is, and God is not. Chapters 3 and 4 to some extent mirror Chapters 1 and 2, on the self and self-less. We begin with a deconstruction of God and consider what it means to be God-less and some of the political and spiritual possibilities that arise from God-lessness. We then explore the possibilities of bringing attention to the mystery of God and asserting the possibility that God is both a slave and the means of our liberty. To claim that God is a slave may seem a shocking assertion, so we will take our time getting there.

There are various well-rehearsed arguments in favour of the belief in God and at least as many carefully thought through arguments against the same. Both parties take belief very seriously. The desire to rationally explain or declaim something is a feature of modernity rather than a timeless or universal quest for truth. Truth is something to be experienced rather than a position to be explained in contradiction to others. Truth is much more enjoyable than correctness. This chapter will briefly tour some of the different forms of theism and atheism in order to illustrate the limitations of both and invite both parties to put aside their orthodoxies in favour of participating in mystery. All orthodoxies are idols of one kind or another and they set up people against each other. This book is for the religious and non-religious, the theist, agnostic and atheist, because mysticism does not rely on belief but rather on an ethic that is grounded in spiritual practice. An activist can call herself an atheist and still be enchanted by what some call God as long as God is not something to be believed in, but rather a space in which we take part in mystery, society and love.

There are probably as many ways of understanding theism – belief in the existence of God – as there are theists but we can still talk in fairly broad categories without committing too many sins of generalization. There is the sort of theism that underpins belief in God from rational or philosophical argument which is sometimes called 'natural law'. This type of theism is a relatively recent popular approach to arguing in favour of there being a god or gods. Some people might argue from design in one way or another or from the observable human quest for meaning. These arguments are compelling. However, people who are convinced by reasoned arguments are usually people who have already had an experience that they discerned to be 'of God' and are looking to defend this experience with a post-Enlightenment or modernist argument. People argue from natural law to defend the supernatural experience that implicitly frames the argument. But there are problems with this approach. First of all, it holds no water for anyone who does not want to be convinced: any argument that can be stitched together by one person can also be unpicked by another. A rationalistic argument for God is a house of cards. Another way of putting this is 'God of the gaps'. Reasoned theists see gaps in scientific knowledge and seek to fill these mysteries with evidence of God's intervention. But science keeps on closing gaps down. Second, it can lead to a sort of functional atheism where the reasoned God we believe in is the God of reason, and since we cannot observe the God of reason at work, a part of us, not too far from consciousness, knows this God to be another idol. So a theism that relies on reason is really atheism with God pegged onto the front of it. Such theists can argue that God exists but each plank of their argument only further reveals its atheistic foundations.

For some of us this reasonable God that leaves us full of unsettled contradictions resolves itself into a kind of deism. Deism was the belief most common among the founding fathers of the USA. It is the belief that God is real but distant and dormant: God was in some way involved in the creation of the universe and there is a source of all things. But this God has now left us to it because there are no miraculous interventions in the material world. It is a convenient position because it demands nothing in terms of argument or action and cannot be proven either way. Functional atheism again.

A third form of theism argues not from reason but from revelation. Arguing God's existence from revelation is no easier than arguing God's existence from reason. Each assertion of revelation is contradicted by any number of others and each revelation conceals and confuses as much as it reveals. In an increasingly globalized world, revelations of God become competitive or relativized experiences. We each find that our revelation is particular to us but need not be true for others. Were we to do an audit of revealed attributes of God we would come unstuck. One revelation may tell us that God is love, another that God demands a genocide. One revelation asserts that God is powerful. Another demonstrates the powerlessness of God. Another functional atheism. The most ardent fundamentalist, of any religion, who professes to believe in the revelations of their sacred texts must live with these revelatory contradictions. This means that they become functional atheists who demand others believe in a god they are afraid to scrutinize, because they subconsciously know it to be a house of cards.

So much for theism then; it does not seem to be a reliable recipe for contemplation or social action. To be an enchanted activist it is not enough to believe in God and have good reason to do so. Such a belief will eventually run aground on the rocky shores of lived reality. It is little wonder that failure to find a way of being spiritual to animate the desire to act is a larger cause of burnout among activists than failure to bring about political change.

The absence of God

Returning to our atheist who may or may not disbelieve in the Protestant God, it is reasonable to say that without theism no one would feel the need to describe themselves as an atheist. Biologist and science apologist Richard Dawkins is often described by others as a 'militant atheist'. There is a particular type of atheism that is quite deliberately modernist: rationalism and reason are the benchmarks of what is real and objectively true. This genre of atheism offers the same comfort of certainty as some types of theism. For the modern atheist, like Richard Dawkins or the late Christopher Hitchens, this is a certainty of method; namely the scientific method. I am not going to spend any time on this type of atheism because, while it leaves room for enchantment, it is not enchanting in itself.

I have met a fair few atheists with sympathy for faith-based approaches to justice. Given the opportunity, most people are willing to think and speak deeply together and find a common language and experience, regardless of whether they are people of faith or people of good faith. This is a generous and sympathetic sort of atheism that allows for the goodness in their religious friends and sees the value in the rituals they perform and the social justice they commit to. I am not going to spend any time on this benign type of atheism either. This kind of atheism is friendly but not, in and of itself, life-giving. Friendly atheists find their joys from other sources, not from their atheism.

Instead of the militant and the benign atheists we are going to explore the possibilities found in an atheism rooted in contemplation of God. One of our most heroic companions on this journey into God-less devotion is the early twentieth-century mystic Simone Weil. Weil was a French Jew who found her spiritual home in the Roman Catholic Church; she studied the ancient Greek philosophers and Indian scriptures and wrestled with the religious and philosophical ideas of her own era.

But she was not only an academic. Simone Weil was also an activist. Weil could almost be said to have been born an activist, agitating both herself and others for the sake of the world as it should be. Aged six, she refused to eat sugar in solidarity with soldiers on the Western front who could not get any. When she embarked on her career as a philosophy teacher during the early 1930s, she refused to heat her room and lived in the equivalent poverty as those without work, giving her wages to the strike funds for workers struggling for their rights. She spent a year in abysmal factory conditions to better understand the alienation of factory work and even joined the Spanish anarchists in their civil war against the fascists. This latter experiment in solidarity turned out to be a complete disaster. Simone Weil was a rubbish soldier and was eventually discharged with an injury when she accidentally walked into a pot of boiling water in a fire pit. This was all the excuse her comrades needed to send her packing.

But Weil was perfectly at home with her imperfections and incompleteness – even if those things frustrated her plans – because for her only God was the perfect fullness of all things. She found God so overwhelming that God's overt presence was destructive, making God's act of withdrawing the primordial creative act. 'God could only create by hiding himself. Otherwise there would be nothing but himself,'[8] she writes, much like the withdrawing of the tide is an act that creates the shore. Weil goes as far as to say that, 'of two men who have no experience of God, he who denies him is perhaps nearer to him than the other.'[9]

God is only known in absent-mindedness. The act of loving is not a self-aware act. Giving full attention to the act of love renders it invisible to the actor.[10] When my youngest daughter was a baby, she would toy with her mum's ear while she was being fed. The habit stayed with her for years afterwards and to some extent is still there. She quickly extended the practice to me. I would watch her eyes while she took hold of my ear and explored it with her tiny fingers. She was utterly attending to the task. It seemed obvious to the watcher that – in that moment – there was no toddler, no fingers and no ear. She didn't think, 'This is a nice ear' or 'I'm enjoying this ear.' Those superficial separations had collapsed into the moment. And it left me like a deer in headlights too. I was hooked! It brings a new definition to the saying 'I am all ears,' I think. In that moment I and the whole universe were 'all ears'. For Simone Weil we can only exist in God's absence, and we can only know God and be known by God in our own absence: when we are obliterated by God's presence.

This is dramatic language, but it chimes with the notion that the self is socially constructed and we are at our happiest when we lose ourselves in the object of our affections or energies. But more than that it asserts that any concept we have of God is false except for the one that we are incapable of analysing, because the moment we do so we lose it. Like a tightrope walker we cannot both trust the rope and look at the rope to see it is there: the moment we do we plummet. This observation is not just vital for the religiously minded, although it has particular implications for those of us who are. We can all form idolatrous attachments that we adore, in some sense. The ability to see these objects of our worship as objects, and not God, frees us to make use of the concept of God as a tool for evaluating our reality and bringing about social change. But before we do that we need to digger deeper into the concept of God-lessness.

4

Reclaiming God

William Blake (1757–1827) is perhaps most famous for writing the words that became the hymn 'Jerusalem', which begins 'And did those feet, in ancient time, walk upon England's mountains green...?' This is a rhetorical question. Blake was an artist, an engraver by trade, and in the poem *Milton* from which this hymn is taken he cries out against the tyranny of the codification of justice that was taking place among the rulers and academics in their 'satanic mills' of establishment religion and morality that weave together abstract ideas of justice. At the time when Blake was writing, in the early nineteenth century, he witnessed the gradual replacement of contextual common law with universal ideas of crime and punishment. Justice was becoming something that could be universally applied and executed. William Blake ironically appropriated Isaiah's utopian vision to drive home his point. In his beautiful and hyperbolic vision, Isaiah concludes, 'The wolf and the lamb shall feed together, the lion shall eat straw like the ox' (Isaiah 65.25). For Blake the belief that we can and apply justice universally, rather than in context and relationship, is an act of oppression. Both God and justice have been misused by us when we think we can pin down what they are in some abstract way. Both God and justice are relational rather than creedal. To work for justice is to work for right relationships; this is a dynamic activity because relationships are never fixed. This task cannot be done from the mistaken idea that we believe in God rather than take part in the divine. We make relational space and God fills it. But that space is always on the move and changing shape.

As activists we must reclaim God from the believer and instead enter into the spiritual practice of participating in the divine. Belief in God is an illusion of knowledge, but participation, God-shaped spirituality, is a transforming ethic that reorients our relationship with God, the universe and one another. When we recognize God in one another and in the space between us, our acts of violence become weightier and our goodness becomes relational rather than legal. We reclaim God, because by doing so we reclaim justice from the generalist and dictator who fixes an imposed morality on their neighbour.

When I first went to India at the age of 18, I was taught a little bit of Hindi. The two most important phrases I learnt were, 'Sorry, I don't speak Hindi very well,' said in a slight panic, and 'Namaste'. Namaste or Namaskar is a word almost universally recognized in India as a greeting. The greeting is accompanied by palms together and pointed upward from the heart. The best interpretation of the spirit of this greeting is, 'That which is of God in me recognizes that which is of God in you.' Quakers call this 'the divine spark' that inhabits each person and is the foundation of Quaker pacifism. In the moment when two people meet, instead of greeting one another, they greet divinity in one another, allowing the self to put aside all prejudices about the other and see only God.

This is a useful exercise if we have experienced the absence of God as well as God's presence. That is to say, the divine that we recognize in one another is not a thing that exists but is beyond both being and knowing. In this sense, there is no God, but there is God. As Simone Weil writes, 'What is the problem?' Knowing, experientially, the absence of God allows us to recognize it in ourselves and others with as little clutter as possible. For Simone Weil this oneness of the two human beings who face each other provides a vital clause in her pacifist ethic. In one of her notes on ethics and violence, she writes:

> Supposing the life of X…were linked with our own so that the two deaths had to be simultaneous, should we still wish him to die? If with our whole body and soul we desire life and if nevertheless without lying, we can reply 'yes', then we have the right to kill.[11]

If we see both that the separation of one self and another is just an illusion but also that the separation of the divine within each by each is also imaginary then we cannot harm or kill another human being without also having done the same to ourselves.

There are some useful analogies, both old and new, that help us grasp our lack of understanding of God. The most famous of these is the story of a group of people who discover an elephant in the dark:

A band of people arrive in the market square in the dark and come across an object that they can't make sense of. The first person reaches out and grabs the elephant's ear: 'Clearly, this is a rug that's been hung out by someone.' The second grabs a tusk: 'How can you think it's a rug?! It's obviously a spear.' A third person grabs at the elephant's leg and replies, 'But surely it's a tree? I can feel the trunk.' By this time, I imagine, the elephant is wondering what on earth is going on but the people groping around in the dark are relentless in their groping and arguing about what it is they each experience.

We cannot see fully, and what little we know about God we reliably misunderstand. We describe our experiences well, but we understand them poorly. None of us can talk meaningfully about God. When I was eight years old, I loved watching a TV series called *The Invisible Man*. I'm not saying that God is an invisible man: stay with me. I remember two things that were odd about the invisible man: first, he was unusually grumpy and second, he wore bandages and sunglasses which seemed to defeat the whole point of being invisible. It might have been more nuanced than that but – hey! – I was only eight. He was invisible, but when he wore bandages, sunglasses and a hat and coat, you could see him. But you couldn't really see him, just the bandages and so on. We wrap God up in our sacred texts, rituals and experiences, and these things help us discern the presence of the divine. But in the end all we really know for certain is our sacred texts, rituals and experiences. These are not to be confused with God, and yet so often they are. These things both conceal and reveal God at the same time. In fact, they can only reveal God by the act of concealing.

Finally and most usefully, there is the analogy of dance. Someone can describe a 'Barnaby' to me as energetic and fun, but they aren't talking about a person but rather a series of organized relationships between humans set to music: a dance. The dance is not the people or the movements any one of them makes. In a sense, the dance is the space between the people who take part. This is what should be positively meant by a 'God of the gaps'. God is hosted, rather than discerned, in the space between 'You' and 'I'. This analogy offers a direct challenge to the individualistic spirituality and piety that are so popular today. We construct God from the shadowy shapes of our shared experience, and these shadows are animated – given spirit – and reveal God to us. Since the dance is always changing so too is the revelation, hence the contradictions that we endlessly face in our quest to find God. Believing in God is pointless, participating in God is divine.

One of the reasons the Jewish sacred texts, the Old Testament, have been such a powerful resource for so many thousands of years is that they are so full of this dance of God. There are two particular dances that we find in the Old Testament. The best is the dance of the slave-class, whose God is counter to all the other dances prevalent at the time. These are people who have been oppressed, crushed and herded around by the elite. They find a god in the gaps who needs neither food (animal sacrifice) nor shelter (temples) but is a source of liberation and justice for the poorest and a sign of hope for a new world in which everyone is free and at peace. It was this slave community – the Hebrews – who gave the ancient Near East the cosmic God who created all things out of nothing and is more powerful and self-resourcing than any other gods. Eventually, through coups and revolts, these people became powerful and their dance began to change to one of conservatism and privilege. The new elite remembered the steps of the old dance and decided to keep the cosmic God but make it a God who demands obedience, who is all powerful, jealous and desiring of sacrifice. The whole of the Old Testament is an interweaving of these two dances. I really like how urban theologian Andrew Parker puts it:

> This change essentially meant getting rid of an ideological god who represented the marginals' clear-sighted and easily checkable way of seeing things and replacing him

with a religious god who represented the blinkered vision of those in authority, whose commands had to be obeyed blindly and without question simply because he was a religious god.[12]

These two dances do not resolve themselves in the New Testament but continue to contend for our attention as the gospels and letters of the early Church continue to wrestle with the ethic of solidarity with the poorest over against the possibility of replacing those who laud it over the nations with their own Christian tyranny.

Since the 1960s and a resurgence of what is called 'liberation theology' in Latin America, we have seen this dance – participation in the God of the margins. Most disagreements between religious groups today amount to people dancing to two very different tunes. Right belief is no longer the point of spirituality; for those who are at the sharp end of social injustice it is ethical practice that tells us what or who God is. There must be a question asked about whether these gods are real since they are constructed by the gaps between us: the social and political systems that govern our lives and that we may think of as spiritual realities. Are these gods real or are they bandages? If they are the latter do they give definition to actual divinity or are they just draped over the indescribable? In discovering the dance moves have we discovered something we can authentically call God, or is it just our imagination? God is in the constant asking of the question, but also in being part of the dance. It is not possible to know God except to participate in the chaos that is the many different dances that go on all at once in the world. Unless we generate the spaces in which God's shape might be discovered, we'll never know the answer. Equally, it is impossible to stand outside the dance and ever know the answer to these important questions. We must *act* to be enchanted, and we must *be* enchanted to keep on dancing.

The enchanted heretic

An enchanted activist holds lightly to creeds and dogmas and so is able to work playfully with the given and constructed ideas of God. This allows activists to recognize all human conceptions of gods as ultimately false, which means we can denounce the false gods that justify the status quo. This makes us heretics or iconoclasts: we smash the idols that demand scapegoats and sacrifice to make room for a more fluid and critical understanding of the divine.

One of my favourite heretics was my good friend John Hull. John Hull died in 2015 aged 80, and in his later years he was an academic second and an activist first. After he retired, he went to work for Queen's Foundation in Birmingham to train Anglican and Methodist church leaders to be activists too. The year before I arrived there he and others had blockaded the port at Faslane where nuclear-armed submarines are docked. Some yearly actions were established among the students, including a public lamentation for the Iraq re-occupation and an annual anti-consumerist carol singing event where staff and students gave out mince pies to passing shoppers and invited them to join in. Here's one of my favourites:

(Tune: God Rest Ye Merry Gentlemen)

Slow down ye frantic shoppers
for there's something we must say:
Big business has been telling us
what Christmas means today.
But we believe there's more to life
than how much you can pay:

Now it's time we decided for ourselves,
for ourselves,
Yes it's time we decided for ourselves.

To some folks Christmas means a time
for gathering with friends
And enemies might take it as
a time to make amends
But TV says it's time for pricey gifts
and selfish ends:

Now it's time we decided for ourselves,
for ourselves,
Yes it's time we decided for ourselves.

Some people feel that Christmas
is when Jesus makes a call
For others it's a time to stress
good will and peace to all
But advertisers tell us it means
Santa's at the mall:

Now it's time we decided for ourselves,
for ourselves,
Yes it's time we decided for ourselves.[13]

We put the word around that we were going to hold an 'anti-consumerist carol singing' event next to the large statue of a bull in the Bull Ring shopping centre. It was just seven of us that first year, and we chose the Bull Ring partly because it was the busiest shopping area in the town, but also because a few of us were angry about the privatization of our city centres: buskers, *Big Issue* sellers and anyone who wanted to be spontaneous in public had been pushed out of these once community-owned spaces, and we wanted to reclaim that space, if only for a little while. But, not wanting any aggravation, we decided that if security asked us to move on we would. I was expecting us to last all of five minutes. Things went well, with a few people taking leaflets from us explaining what we were doing but not many stopping to listen. We managed half an hour before I noticed four security guards hovering in the distance: just watching and talking on their radios to the invisible boss.

Eventually one walked up to me, since I was giving out the leaflets, and asked, 'Excuse me, do you have permission to be here?'

'We're singing carols!' I cheerfully replied.

'I'm afraid I'm going to have to ask you to leave.'

I shrugged and nodded. Just as I was about to head back to our group and tell them the game was up, he asked, 'And are they with you?'

Remembering our original plan was not to leave until we were asked by security, what could I say?

'Err…no; no they're not. You'll have to ask each one of them to leave separately. Sorry.'

This bought us another five minutes during which passers-by were grabbing leaflets off me quicker than I could give them out.

If you fancy doing something like this yourself, we've since learned a few lessons and have developed the action

- Calling it 'anti-consumerist' puts all sorts of people off who would otherwise get involved. 'Alternative carol singing' communicates perfectly well.

- It's good to have costumes, brass instruments and drums.

- Chocolate money is never a bad idea.

- If we have contacts in the press, this sort of thing makes their day – they are as sick of saccharine Christmas as the rest of us.

- Instead of giving out leaflets we give out carol sheets, so our group grows as we sing. These sheets include debt advice and ideas for home-made or free Christmas presents.

- Try not to do this near to local market stall holders. They have enough to deal with. A pitch between a few large corporations is better. Outside a pay-day lender shop is best of all.

- It is always nice to go for a cuppa together afterwards to laugh about what happened and share thoughts, feelings and ideas.

- Advertise an hour – you can always sing for longer if you want to.

- Don't be discouraged if the first year you do this you attract small numbers (although if you're a better organizer than me you might have more). This sort of thing builds with time and effort.

- Above all, have fun with it. Justice and compassion can put the 'merry' back into 'merry Christmas'.

For John Hull this action gave him a great opportunity to 'blaspheme the money god', but he also offers a whole raft of other ways to do this. Below is an edited version of his previously unpublished thoughts on the matter:

- Money loves money, and money is attracted to money. We do the opposite. Instead of getting we start giving. Every time you give freely you shake the throne of the money god.

- Everything, we say, has its price. Let us break the exchange thing by giving away our unwanted stuff.

- The money god loves vagueness and secrecy. How many bankers do you hear being interviewed? We encourage openness. We don't secretly store up money, except to give someone a nice surprise. We don't boast about having more than we actually have or tell lies about having less money than we really have. This is part of what John meant when he wrote, 'If we walk in the light as God is in the light, we have fellowship with one another' (1 John 1.7).

- The money god is a self-deceiver and encourages people to deceive themselves. We take steps to avoid self-deception about money. Know what proportion of your income you give. It is easy to have an inflated idea of this. If you work it out, it may not be as much as you fondly imagine.

- Finally, the money god is utterly selfish. We are encouraged to think that our money is really ours but the truth is all money is social. We don't think of our money as ours but as belonging to the community.

A great example of the third of these heresies is practised by the Iona Community, who work out of the ancient abbey on the Scottish island of Iona, with members all over the world. The members meet regularly in regional groups and pledge to be fully open about all their finances with one another. They do not choose to hold everything in common but they do choose to hold everything in honest transparency. Some have more money than others and they are able to talk openly about this without judgement but with a mutual challenge. By being open and non-attached to their finances all of them have learnt a new way of being with one another in which money is not a metric of worth but something to hold lightly to until another needs it. This is powerful and blasphemous stuff and shows we can all have the courage to be a bit more heretical every day.

Heresy is a great tool of activist spirituality. How we choose to commit heresy is up to us. In 2013 I took part in two acts of heresy against the idol of war. In June I went with five co-conspirators to RAF Waddington in Lincolnshire. RAF Waddington is where British drones are piloted from. At the time of our blasphemous action RAF drones were flying over Afghanistan, killing and traumatizing children, who had to listen to the constant droning of warplanes above their communities, even as they tried to sleep at night. These drones have killed many civilians. We don't know how many because the Ministry of Defence will only admit to a few. But the United States Air Force has admitted to hundreds, so the true British figure is likely to be much higher than official records suggest. Early one Monday morning, six people of different faiths or of good faith cut through the fence at RAF Waddington to make a 'gateway of peace' into the site. Four of the six went deeper into the site to attempt to find the drone pilots and give them messages from the people of Afghanistan. Myself and Susan Clarkson, a Quaker, remained just inside the perimeter to lament our complicity with violence and pray for peace. We planted a vine and a fig tree and made a small shrine with candles, icons and images of civilians killed in airstrikes. The vine and fig tree were allusions to a text in the Bible: 'But they shall sit under their own vine and under their own fig trees; and no one shall make them afraid' (Micah 4.4). After nearly an hour we were approached by RAF and civilian police and were arrested. The police in the UK tend to be polite to quiet protesters, although that does not necessarily translate into kindness. We were held 'incommunicado' for the first 12 hours and were not formally released until 32 hours after we had been arrested. During this time most of our homes were raided by police. They told me they were going to raid my house, and this caused me a lot of worry. Here's the context: most of my congregation did not know where I was and would be shocked to see a bunch of police officers at the vicarage. My wife was out that evening at an orchestra rehearsal, and the children, aged four and six, were at home with a guest asylum seeker who had fled police violence in her own country. I prayed like never before. Soon after 9pm I was allowed a phone call. The guest had been calm and organized and managed to alert a number of people who rushed straight over, including my wife. My elder daughter, on seeing five police officers in flak jackets arrive in our home and start going through all the rooms, decided to follow them around asking questions and telling them why drones are bad. She is awesome. Although she was upset when she saw they'd taken our computers, cameras, posters, notebooks and other stuff, she was not too upset. In fact, when I finally came home, she greeted me with, 'Daddy, Daddy, guess what? The police have been, and your office has never looked so tidy!'

But this was just the beginning of the blasphemy. The congregation held a vigil for peace on the day of our appearance in court. Despite holding a variety of views on the rightness or wrongness of drone warfare they came together in their diversity for the sake of peace and justice. When our day in court came, the judge called us 'dutiful people with a legitimate target' and gave us a token fine for our troubles. We felt hugely vindicated, and of course we generated debate both locally and nationally. For me, this particular act of heresy, in the eyes of the powerful, was never about the public engagement and all about my personal commitment to being a heretic. And by and large it was a joy to do – although anxious and tiring for us all at times.

In September of that same year I went with two members of my church and a priest activist from Leicester diocese to the Defence & Security Equipment International (DSEI) international arms fair in London. Three priests – Helen Hayes, Chris Howson and I – got together with a large group of activists to organize an exorcism. We planned to exorcize the arms fair. We were robed up, and I took with me a thurible for the incense and some blessed water for sprinkling. The Reverend Chris Howson brought the service sheets and led the prayers. The arms fair happens every other year and draws people from all kinds of private companies and nation states; some of the weapons on sale are legal and some are not, some kill and others maim or deliberately torture. What unites them all is the desire to make money from violence. Billions of dollars of profit are made from war every year by big banks and corporations, which are heavily subsidized by the state. In fact, this economy is so heavily subsidized that our government successfully hides the fact that, for tax-paying citizens, this is a loss-making enterprise both morally and economically.

We arrived at the entrance to the conference centre where a 'die-in' had just taken place. As I arrived, I saw a friend – Siobhan – being carted off by police, which was annoying, because I hadn't had a chance to say 'hello' and catch up. As we squatted down on a small traffic island, I fished out a disc of charcoal from my pocket and tried to light it. But, fool that I am, I had not brought any tongs to hold the charcoal and kept burning my fingers. I muttered under my breath, 'If only my sacristan was here.' Immediately the woman standing next to me looked down at me and said, 'I'm a sacristan; here, give it to me.' Somehow she managed to get the charcoals glowing brightly without burning her fingers or dropping anything. Thank God there was an expert just when I needed one.

We processed into the road and began our exorcism of the arms fair. It was a powerful and moving experience both for those involved and for the many hundreds who watched and protected us from the police. I lost count of the number of times we were threatened with arrest as we performed the ceremony: a line of police stood directly in front of me and were not keen on me trying to use the holy water. I'm so glad they did not notice that the object in my other hand was smoking heavily. We were polite and friendly to the officers at all times, letting them know exactly how long our action would take and that we would leave as soon as were done. We made it clear to them that we recognized their desire to arrest us but suggested to them it might be counter-productive.

'Get off the road or you will be arrested.'

'I understand that you are going to arrest us; that's up to you, of course, but if you wait ten minutes we will leave after that.'

'Leave right now, or I WILL arrest you.'

'We're not going to leave yet, but we will leave when we've finished our prayers.'

And so on, and so on. In fact, if there was any heated arguing it was between the police as they argued about what to do with us. So often protests turn into a bad pantomime with blue-collar police officers up against angry protestors. All sense of purpose is lost for both sides. But our issue was not primarily with them and we were not there to protest so much as to blaspheme the God of war and pray for peace. We did, so we went home.

Emptying God

All great religious and social reformers have been heretics of one form or another. Perhaps you could say they had an orthodoxy that was not common to their time. These were people who found the dances of their generation had turned into marches: they chose to step out of line.

Rabi'a al-Adawiya was a Sufi saint from eighth-century Basra, who lived in poverty and challenged greed, hypocrisy and male power. She once walked along a street in Basra holding a torch in one hand and a pail of water in the other. Asked why, she replied, 'I want to put fire to paradise and pour water over hell, so that these two veils disappear and it becomes plain who venerates God for love and not for fear of hell or hope for paradise.'[14]

Or you might think of the Buddha, Jesus, or the Indian reformer and agitator B.R. Ambedkar, all of whom challenged the spiritual and social domination systems of their times with a new way of being human.

I want to finish this chapter by focusing on the traditions that have arisen around Jesus of Nazareth, both in the Bible and in the Church, since this is where my own activism is most enchanted. In fact, of all the activists in the human story there isn't another I find more enchanting or inspiring, so I had better give him some attention!

One of the earliest recorded Christian hymns was quoted or written by the apostle Paul in his letter to the church in Philippi:

Christ, though in the image of God,
didn't deem equality with God
something to be clung to –
but instead became completely empty
and took on the image of oppressed humankind:
born into the human condition,
found in the likeness of a human being.
Jesus was thus humbled –
obediently accepting death, even death on a cross!
Because of this, God highly exalted Christ
and gave to Jesus the name above every other name,
so that at the name of Jesus every knee must bend
in the heavens, on the earth, and under the earth,
and every tongue proclaim to the glory of God:
Jesus Christ reigns supreme!

(PHILIPPIANS 2.6–11)[15]

Think back to the story of how the Jewish idea of God was first shaped by their Hebrew ancestors who longed for liberation and saw their god as more truly God than any of the deities that, in various ways, represented the ideology of the powerful. The Hebrew God of slaves was a cosmic god above all others who did not need anything to subsist. But this cosmic god was gradually co-opted by a new power elite and the dance of liberation became a march of colonial power. When Paul says that 'every knee must bend', he is not referring to the poor and the powerless. They are already on bended knee under the brutal power of the Roman Empire. The apostle Paul is singing about the powerful elite: the kings, princes, Caesars and their representatives, who bow for each other or for no one. The Jesus described in the Bible reclaims the idea of the God of slaves, and he does this by reorganizing social and spiritual life around a new community and an ancient set of ethics.

In a sense the role of the activist is to summon God by joining with others to build an altar, tabernacle or whatever word you might use for describing the process of bringing about new ways that people can relate to one another more deeply and justly. John's Gospel starts off by saying that, in Jesus, God 'pitched a tent among us', the tent being a symbol of God's presence in the midst of the community. But many of the activities traditionally ascribed to Jesus are clearly the work of a team of people, rather than some lone activist. Barbara Glasson, who founded the pioneering 'bread church' in Liverpool and is currently weaving together communities in Bradford, writes and talks about 'prophetic communities' rather than 'prophets'. It is communities which are pushed to the margins themselves that reveal the Hebrew God: the God who acts on us and who causes us to act for justice. Among some contemporary followers of Jesus there is a great deal of talk about the idea of Jesus returning. In the Bible there is a story that, if taken literally, can seem rather odd, which has Jesus floating up into the sky. In this story, Jesus, who has been raised from the dead, takes the disciples outdoors and says goodbye to them before being taken up to 'heaven' in a cloud. In the Greek world the same word is used for sky and heaven. It's *ouranos*, and it is where we get the planetary name 'Uranus' from. The apostle Paul wrote about Jesus returning in the same way, and so some Christians believe that Jesus will float back down from the sky one day. Let's park that literalism where it belongs, eh? Jesus returns in that space between 'I' and 'thou'; that is, 'heaven', and we create heaven when we work together for justice and peace. We are re-enchanting our world, when we do anything to rebuild and reorganize human relationships to be deeper and broader than they currently are: we conjure God.

In Chapter 1, we reflected on the Greek philosophical idea that we 'never step into the same river twice' and how that illustrates the fluid nature of self. The same might be said to be true of the divine. Whether or not you affirm a constant divine reality somewhere, to try to experience that reality in the same way more than once is impossible. Both our understanding of reality and reality itself are endlessly changing. Once when I went swimming in a river in North Wales, I saw that someone had built a fence across the river. Whether there was some sensible reason for this I cannot fathom, but it was probably important. What it did not do was stop or change the river's flow. This is what creeds are like in comparison to the deeper reality of God. Religions set up lists of 'correct beliefs' to fence in God, but God just tumbles past them like they barely exist. This is what happens to fixed beliefs: they give way or they get destroyed by the nimble otherness of God. Enchanted activism is being with God, invoking God, relating in the presence of God to others in ways that challenge the accepted gods of the world. We make a space for the divine by joining with others to create a just space for human flourishing.

5

Re-enchanting Religion

'Religion' is so often a dirty word, not least among activists. The UK has mostly turned its back on organized religion, and activists can see how often it is used to pacify citizens: the very opposite of activism. For Karl Marx it was the 'opiate of the people', and for Emma Goldman, the mother of anarchist thought and practice, it was a tool of state oppression. They were not wrong. Yet whenever I go to demonstrations, marches or protests there are always plenty of people of faith, and most of these people are organized with other people of faith on a week-by-week basis. Their faith is nurtured in community and accountability. When I joined with five other people to break into an RAF military base in Lincolnshire, where armed drones were piloted over Afghanistan, five of us were motivated by our faith and were members of religious groups. None of us find being religious easy, yet we have stayed that course for decades of our lives. We need to look at the role of religion in the wellbeing of the activist with new generosity.

If we look honestly at why religion is a problem, then we can also look at why it also has potential to be part of the solution. If God and self are both human constructs then so too is religion, but that does not lower its value. A generous faithfulness of belonging to others can be a radical and liberating stance. I am not necessarily arguing that activists should join traditional religious institutions, although for some of us that is the path we travel. Rather, activists who are enchanted with other people and willing to make a covenant to faithfully travel with others on their spiritual journey to a better world will have a greater impact than those who are not. As an ancient African proverb puts it: if you want to go fast, travel alone, but if you want to go far, travel together.

A couple of years ago I was invited to give a talk to a group of about 40 retired professionals in the ex-mining town of Warsop in Nottinghamshire. They sat in rows, like in a classroom 30 years ago. But we had a great time, and nobody got to be 'teacher'. We discussed the history of fossil fuels and whether our increased reliance on gas and oil has been the cause of every major conflict since the Great War. I wore my clerical collar and was introduced as a church minister, and so my stories were framed, in part, by how they understood what I represented: religion. Most of these men were brought up in a coal-mining town, so they brought their particular perspective to the debate. During the discussion I was challenged by a man who said, 'You talk about fossil fuels, but isn't it really religion that causes all the wars, not capitalism or the state? It's your lot that's the problem!' At this there was a general murmur of agreement, although not total consensus. People often think of church as being for older people – in the UK the average age of a churchgoer is well above the national average age – but in reality older people have also rejected church, and religion is given only an occasional civic role in their lives or is something they consider to be a private matter. For a younger generation, spirituality has never been reliant on organized religion: 'I think of myself as spiritual rather than religious' is a common self-descriptor. According to data published by the think tank Theos in 2013, 34 per cent of 'non-religious' people in the UK believe in some kind of spiritual being. They also note that 52 per cent think spiritual forces have some influence either on people's thoughts or on the natural world. Theos notes that spiritual beliefs are clearly not the preserve of the 'religious' but are to be found across religious and non-religious groups.[16] If Chapters 1 and 2 were about enchanting the self and God, then this chapter is an attempt to re-enchant religion. Some might say this is a far bigger challenge. Religion gets a pretty rough ride of it these days and is seen by many as incompatible with the modern world, and by others as the source of all evil. Such cynicism is understandable, when so much terror and violence has been unleashed on the world by religious groups. In parts of central and east Africa 'The Lord's Resistance Army' torture and kill innocent people in the name of God and the Ten Commandments. In Northern Ireland violence between Protestant and Catholic Christians continues to this day. In Myanmar Buddhist terrorists stranded boatloads of Muslim Rohingyas at sea, where they died of dehydration. Former US president George W. Bush claimed to have been instructed by God to bomb Iraqis, and Al Qaida killed in the name of God too. I have visited Gujarat many times and sat in mosques listening to stories of the atrocities committed against Muslims by Hindus there in 2002: murder, rape, burning people alive. All this in the name of religion.

And yet to be a spiritual person and to be an activist means to be open to letting both our activism and our spirituality be forged in the crucible of common life. Anything else risks becoming spiritual fluff, because it becomes exclusively self-referencing without being tested by community. This is the sort of hobby spirituality that is often comfortable and unchallenged. It rarely leads to spiritual growth. It fails to recognize that there is a spiritual commons in which we all live without the fences of enclosed ethereal beliefs. Privatized spirituality models itself on capitalism's primacy of the selfish individual. Can an activist be spiritual but not religious? Religion is not so irredeemably corrupted that it cannot be a vehicle for social good. Religion has been privatized, domesticated or co-opted by the caste with power over our lives and their dominant narrative. But religion can and should be public, feral, and popular, in that it can belong to ordinary people in their neighbourhoods, working out their spirituality together. As we shall see, both co-opted and popular religion have had times of agency, but when the powers-that-be and the violent monopolize religion it loses its truly radical and social virtues. Just as activists often experiment in community living, common ownership and cooperative labour, so spirituality should be a corporate endeavour with all the difficulties and joys that involves.

The privatization of religion

Privatization of religion, in the form of personal spirituality, is not the only reason people turned away from religion in such huge numbers in recent times. The co-option of religion by those with power over our lives for their own advancement has disillusioned ordinary people who see the religious narrative as illegitimate, disempowering and corrupt. During World War I, for example, the Church of England was largely co-opted by the state to promote a war in which millions of working men were killed at the hands of their incompetent generals. This led to the disillusionment of a generation with authority in general and with the moral authority of religion in particular. For them religion was illegitimate. My research in India has led me to believe that conversion to Christianity pacified rather than empowered the Dalit communities who were looking to escape oppression but were only taught to hide their Dalit identity in their Christian one and put up with the status quo. For them religion was disempowering. Time and again we see religious authorities caught up in scandals regarding money, power, sex and silence on matters of injustice. Religion is seen as self-serving and corrupt, and there is evidence to prove it.

The processes of co-option and privatization of religion have been accelerated at certain points in history. An example of the co-option of religion by a powerful leader in order to use it in order to unify and control people would be the conversion of the Roman emperor Constantine to Christianity. But, since this is co-option we are discussing, it would be more honest to frame the events as the conversion of Christianity to Constantine. Constantine co-opted Christianity and altered it almost beyond recognition for his own ends, but he did not privatize religion, rather he made it a vital public force for governing the people. An example of privatization and co-option of religion together is the so called 'War of Religions' in sixteenth- and seventeenth-century Europe, although radical theologian William Cavanaugh prefers to call them 'the birth pangs of the state'.[17] Both of these examples we will look at in a little more detail below.

For Christianity, co-option by empire goes back further even than that. It began with the fateful Battle of the Milvian Bridge in the year 312. According to legend, Constantine, the emperor of Rome from 312 to 337 CE, saw a vision of a Christian symbol and heard a voice telling him that if he fought under the banner of 'Christ the King', he would be victorious in battle. He did, and he was. By the time of Constantine's death the whole thing had been flipped on its head. Constantine went on to make Christianity a licit religion in the Roman Empire, and pretty soon you could not get on politically or economically without converting to Constantine's Christianity.

Constantine set about clearing up division and disagreement among Christians, by force where necessary. Christianity had never been a single and unified religion – even Jesus' disciples disagreed with each other and with him. Different beliefs and practices rubbed up against each other or existed in self-referencing silos of ideology and practice. But the Roman Emperor formalized the rules about who had authority and what statements of belief could be used in worship. What had been a feral and mobile religion had been fenced in and brought under the patronage of the state. Whereas the early Church had mostly forbidden members to join the Roman army – seeing fighting for Rome as a form of idol worship – under Constantine it became necessary to be a Christian to enlist. If the Roman Empire brought strength and order through violence, then the Christian religion was the decorated glove of respectability that it wore into battle. This period of Western history has been referred to as 'Christendom' and would last through the Middle Ages.

Constantine had taken Christianity into state ownership and fenced it in. Christianity was now a desirable piece of real estate. Anything privatised and fenced in needs to be protected by violent force. Christianity was now a desirable piece of real estate; it would never be the same again. We live with the legacy of this twist in Christianity's fate to this day. In the UK the Church of England, a reformed version of the Catholic faith, still has a great deal of privilege and entitlement. The monarch is crowned by the archbishop of the Church of England, and some of the bishops have an automatic place in the upper house of government. At a local level bishops and priests have informal access to power in all kinds of ways. It is also true to say that Christians make up a huge number of the volunteers in society who work hard and do a great amount of good for their community. This is sometimes used to justify the privileged place that the Church has. But this privileged place is gradually being eroded: from the moral authority of bishops to the relationship between churchgoing and respectability, we are in a period of history sometimes called 'post-Christendom'. Post-Christendom means that Christendom is still alive and well, but not as alive and not nearly as robust as it used to be. It is a confusing time for those accustomed to entitlement; some have adapted and others have not.

There are lots of reasons why post-Christendom happened but a very important one was the battle between the emerging nation states in medieval Europe. The year is 1521, and a radical German monk, with little positional authority but growing influence, stands before the most powerful council of Europe and before the Roman Emperor himself. Among the council stand the princes and rulers of the day, many with huge ambitions and grudges to match. They long to be free from the coercive moral power of the Pope but lack the theological leverage and vision to organize it. The German monk Martin Luther knows this, and since he is in a bit of a fix for spreading ideas that challenged the Pope's authority, he takes a chance. Luther has been invited to defend himself or retract his accusations of corruption that he had publicly posted against the Roman Catholic Church, nailed to the door of Wittgenstein Cathedral. Rather than backing down he decides to look for backers from among the princes to spread his ideas even further. In his long and sophisticated defence of his writing he speaks of the tyranny of the bishop of Rome, which is the Pope, and makes the vital connection between bad theology and evil rule. Luther implies that good Christian rulers do not follow the Pope but follow instead the Bible. He ends his speech with a killer blow: 'I neither can nor will retract anything; for it cannot be right for a Christian to speak against his country.' Genius. Luther knew that some of these secular leaders were looking for a new narrative from which to challenge the power of the public imperial religion. He spotted an opportunity in the changing political landscape, and so did many of his hearers. Many of these leaders chose to back Luther and his mission to reform the Church. So began the Protestant Reformation, not with the Ninety-five Theses of Luther nailed to the door of the cathedral but with that meeting at which he organized the powerful rulers to put the secular sword above the authority of the 'spiritual sword' of Church rule.

The Wars of Religion took place during the sixteenth and seventeenth centuries before which there was no such thing as a nation state. There were people who ruled over territory and its inhabitants, usually in relation to a particular place: a city state, perhaps the region around that city or even a number of regions and ethnic groups might fall under the same person's status as in the earlier-mentioned Roman Empire. A nation state is defined here as power vested in a defined territory itself to which those who live in that territory owe their allegiance that is then ruled on behalf of those people by one form of government or another. Before the development of the nation state, divine status was accorded to rulers, be they religious leaders or secular leaders who are authorized by the Church. Either way, deference was due to the religious rulers in order for secular leaders to legitimize their power. In order to better consolidate their powers the princes of Europe needed to do what Constantine before them had done and choose a banner under which to fight but, like Constantine, they were only really loyal to themselves.

What we now often refer to as the 'Wars of Religion' was in reality a war between religious authority and secular authority. The reason it is now framed as an outbreak of disorder, driven by religious disagreement but pacified by secular rulers, is simply that the state won out. The victors always get to write the history books. Those who I call secular leaders were also religious people with convictions based on faith but they were secular in that, until this point, they derived their power from the institutions of the Church indirectly and used that power to organize the aspects of life we normally think of as secular: the markets, war, transport and administration of government generally.

Charles V, the Holy Roman Emperor (Catholic), fought the Lutherans from 1547 to 1555, but the Lutherans were supported by French Catholics. If that was a war between two competing religious ideologies, then you would not expect to find Catholics fighting Catholics. Again, between 1618 and 1648, a war in Spain aimed at consolidating a newly emerging nation state under the Catholic banner but relied on a Lutheran ruler to conquer Bohemia. It was opposed by Catholic princes and routed by Swedish Protestants funded by French Catholics. In the final 13 years of this 30-year war it became a battle between two Catholic dynasties: the Bourbons and the Habsburgs. Clearly these were not wars fought on the basis of religion, but the two biggest winners were the emergence of the nation state as the holder of all public moral authority and the privatization of religion. The state now held the divine status of protector of the people, especially from religious fundamentalism. This role implicitly elevated nation states to replace the divine status formally held by rulers and dynasties. From now on, the Church, of every denomination, would have to kneel to the prince and not vice versa. The liberal necessity of the privatization of religion was argued on the basis that religion was too dangerous to be free and must be kept in check by the benign authority of the state. After all, no one wants another set of wars of religions, eh? Historians may persist in calling these wars the 'Wars of Religion' to give the state justification for its violent birth. But an activist who accepts religion as the scapegoat for state violence has missed the point entirely.

Through the ascendancy of the state in Europe in the seventeenth century, religion was successfully domesticated and privatized. The evangelical revivals of the nineteenth and early twentieth century reinvigorated and democratized folk religion but at the same time gave further weight to the idea that faith is about individual assent to doctrine and private piety. It did nothing to challenge the idol of the divine status of the nation state, but rather reinforced that status with the focus on individual salvation. By and large the Catholic and reformed churches fell in line with this approach to religion as a private matter of personal piety more than public ethics. This image of religion persists to this day. In the last year I was invited to debate with an MP who insisted that the church should 'stay out of politics' and sent an email by a county councillor who told me Christians should not be naïvely meddling with stuff that was 'none of our business'. I hear this a lot, perhaps you do too.

The process of seeing nation states being birthed through violence that expresses itself through religion is repeated today as conflicts in the Middle East see groups like Daesh, sometimes called ISIS, attempting to erase Sykes–Picot state boundaries created by Anglo-French colonialists at the end of the Great War in an attempt to control the region and its resources. Popular discourse is separating Muslims into two kinds: moderates and fundamentalists. Moderates understand the role of religion as subservient to the state which has supreme, God-like privilege. Moderates practise their faith without interfering with other people's lives. Fundamentalists see the state as subservient to God and seek to bring about God's will through violence. In reality, religious people need to grow in confidence that their spirituality is not separate from their public ethic. It is entirely appropriate for Muslims in any country to be angry about the way Western colonialists have shaped and exploited some Arab regions. In the UK it is increasingly difficult for Muslims to speak out against state-sponsored violence and injustice, and our government has put together a 'Prevent' strategy that tells Muslim children in schools what they can and cannot think or say. Violence that originated in revolt against the collapsing colonial project is being projected onto the religious communities to put them in their place and use them as scapegoats for a violent world. The state takes sacrifices of lives and offerings of money and demands obedience from us in exchange for protection, justice and prosperity. The state is one of the most powerful Gods of our age and patriotism is its religion. To have a critique of religion without a critique of patriotism risks missing the possibility that religion can be an expression of prophetic denunciation of the idolization of the state.

Rootless religion

If domestication by the state is one cause of the privatization of religion, then the increasing mobility of human societies is another. A mobile person requires a mobile religion that they can pack up in a bag and unpack in a new place. Three major causes of human displacement are the labour market, war and climate change. For rich and poor alike, the labour market demands a mobile work force. Human labour is at the whim of the free market and must move for work or starve. Social mobility looks like freedom, but it is nothing of the kind. Increased flooding, famine and drought cause mass migrations and the associated political instability which, together with interference by global powers, leads to wars.

All three forces of movement overlap, of course. The reality of this is not too far away from where I live. It takes me just four hours to drive to Folkestone and get a 40-minute train to Calais. I have been visiting the refugee camp there with refugees now located in Britain and activists and faith leaders from across the UK. It is an improvised and chaotic refugee camp which its residents call 'the Jungle'. The inhabitants of the Jungle come from all over the world. Most are from Afghanistan, Egypt, Eritrea, Ethiopia, Iran, Iraq, Libya, Sudan and Syria. These are countries undergoing conflict caused by government, external corporations and warring factions often fuelled by drought and famine. Various protection racketeers and slave-smugglers operate in the camp, especially at night, but also openly during the day. Just to pitch a tent in the camp costs money at the threat of force. Calais is a cold and windswept place. The wind that whips across the camp is bitter and sharp with grit.

Between the tents are pools of stagnant water and rubbish from fly-tippers. Foot disease and lung infections are all too common. Many of the refugees have travelled across several borders to get as far as this desperate place. I asked a refugee who is now a community organizer why people take such risks. 'There are three reasons,' he told me, 'blood, sweat and tears.' Blood: I have family at home that I need to support and relatives in Britain who have offered to help me. Sweat: I have been promised work. I speak some English, so I hope to study or find a job in the UK. Tears: my home has been destroyed, and there is no hope, no food and no future for me back at home. Blood, sweat and tears have been moving people on from place to place for thousands of years.

But amidst the despair there are organized and talented people determined to honour something of themselves on their journey. Mosques and churches have been built and cared for. On one of our visits we were joined by an Ethiopian Orthodox priest. Together we visited the Church of St Michael and All Angels built by Eritrean and Ethiopian refugees using donated wood and tarpaulin and decorated inside with skill and care. We gathered together inside, Christians, Jews and Muslims, and prayed together for an end to this injustice. I was reminded of the Psalms written by the Jewish people when they were removed from Israel and taken to work for the Babylonian empire over 2000 years ago:

By the rivers of Babylon
  there we sat down and there we wept
  when we remembered Zion.
On the willows there
  we hung up our harps.
For there our captors
  asked us for songs,
and our tormentors asked for mirth, saying,
  'Sing us one of the songs of Zion!'
How could we sing the Lord's song
  in a foreign land?
If I forget you, O Jerusalem,
  let my right hand wither!

(PSALMS 137.1–5)

Their worship was framed by their relationship with a particular place, focused on a temple and a city. In captivity they lamented both the loss of that place but also the loss of their capacity for religious comfort and strength. While many people successfully transport their religion from place to place, something happens to them and their map of reality in the process. Their religion becomes portable instead of rooted in the place that brought it into being. It means that religions are also becoming increasingly sectarian, distinguishing clusters of cultural and linguistically defined groups from one another, instead of creating a commonality of local expression.

The market creates mobility of the religious but then mobility also creates a market for religion as religious identities meet and contend in new public spaces. If an individual's religious identity has no bearing on their covenant with other people on whom they depend for mutual flourishing then it becomes a private faith interchangeable according to context. While there is no straightforward solution to this, the need for diverse civic institutions to come together regularly for the common good is vital to the re-grounding of displaced people in new contexts. We can decorate this commodification of religion in the language of personal choice but this is just another idol to be blasphemed. Personal choice is not the source of our salvation: it often atomizes us, generating a selfish and fragmented society. Far from being our salvation, personal choice dams us to social hell. That is not to say it is always wise to be faithful to the religious identity that we were born to, or that we should never make personal choices. Your religion does not have the right to abuse or exploit you. But carefully considered faithfulness can be revolutionary in that it allows the activist to work within a spiritual community to refunction it, often against its will, so that it works for and with the most oppressed instead of against them. Religious institutions are full of people with rich stories, strong values and huge motivation to change things. Activists who are not enchanted by this risk are throwing out the baby with the bath water.

Two of the most radical reformers of Western Christian history are Francis of Assisi (1182–1226) and Dorothy Day (1897–1980). Both remained faithful to the religious institutions they belonged to, despite opposition, and in doing so brought about social changes. Francis of Assisi was the wealthy son of a merchant, but he gave up all his riches for a simple life. He formed a community that rebuilt the Church, literally and metaphorically, and took care of those who were neglected and impoverished. With his brothers and sisters in faith he founded the Orders of Friars Minor and their sister community the Order of Saint Clare. Throughout his life Francis was faithful to the Catholic Church and to his orders, but he remained a prophetic voice. By refusing to give up his activism he revealed a far deeper sense of covenant than those who ruled over him. When Pope Innocent III began a campaign against Islam in Jerusalem in 1213, he recruited the whole of Christendom to the fight. Through preaching, money and men were gathered to do 'God's will'. Faith leaders were co-opted, and Innocent's successor, Pope Honorius II, continued the bloodthirsty war. It seems, however, that Francis did not condone the crusades. Having failed to persuade the Church to stop the fighting, he went personally to the Sultan Malik al-Kamil to assure him that the crusades did not represent Jesus' gospel of peace. Francis' commitment to poverty and to learning from and with Muslims led to discord among his own followers and eventually to him being deposed as leader of his own Order. It would have been a straightforward thing for Francis to begin again with a new religion, because his own was so corrupted. But this happened before the fickleness of either modernism or capitalism shaped Western values, and it means that his movement and story continues to act as a prophetic and reforming voice within his own Church to this day.

The religion of Francis was not privatized, and neither was his activism. The same was true of Dorothy Day, a late convert to the Roman Catholic Church. She was an anarchist before her conversion and remained anarchic throughout her life. In the 1930s, in a depressed and impoverished New York, Dorothy Day founded the *Catholic Worker* newspaper and established Houses of Hospitality for those who had lost jobs and homes. Day and her fellow Catholic Workers shared all the labour equally: everyone cleaned the toilets, and everyone shared the big decisions. Many of them, like her, chose to live materially simple lives to avoid paying tax. They did this because they were pacifists and did not want to give money to fund state violence. Because of their hard work and compassion the Catholic Workers in New York were making the Roman Catholic Church look really good, so the bishop was pleased. What the bishop was less pleased about was Day's peace activism. Being nice to people is one thing but standing up for the oppressed is quite another. When the bishop gave Day an ultimatum – pack up your politics or lose my financial support – Day refused to either quit the work *or* the Church. Instead she negotiated: he could leave her to the entirety of her work, or she could take it to the neighbouring diocese. The bishop, wisely, decided to leave her to it. Despite its violence and hypocrisy, Dorothy Day remained faithful to her Roman Catholic religion for the rest of her life, holding the tension between her institution's idiosyncrasies and her own prophetic calling. Her religion enchanted her activism, even if the institution that hosted her religion did not.

In the West, as we have seen, people often say they are 'spiritual but not religious'. This approach to spirituality is a product of capitalist culture just as much as it is a result of a desire to maintain ethical integrity in the face of flawed institutional religion. While the rejection of religion is understandable, activism that maintains corporate faithfulness leads to far greater learning and effectiveness than privatized spirituality ever could. Enchantment with religion leads inevitably to uncomfortable compromises, but we may find we were wrong in our puritanical standards.

Power and religion

When our eldest daughter was a toddler, my wife and I decided to take a ferry to northern Spain and drive our camper van through the Pyrenees and north to Calais, France. It was a trip of incredible adventures and mishaps. We got distracted along the route, of course, and one of the greatest diversions was to Lourdes, a small town in Southern France built around a site of pilgrimage, where in 1858 a young girl – Bernadette Soubirous – was said to have seen visions of Mary. We took in the sights and sounds and in the evening watched the candlelit procession. As dusk gathered, resident pilgrims processed and sang 'Ave Maria!' – 'Honour to Mary'. At the front of the procession were those unable to walk or even sit up who were lying in carts and pulled by volunteers, followed by those in wheelchairs and then those on crutches and finally the able bodied. While I grant this offers a superficial understanding of wellness and says little of the mind, I found it deeply moving. Those least included in society, the most marginalized, had been given the place of honour. The world was turned upside down.

The morning after the candlelit procession we took a walk around the 'Stations of the cross'. These are a series of images – in this case, statues – that tell the story of Jesus' final moments from trial to execution. At the top of the hill at Lourdes is a statue of Jesus nailed to a cross. Beside him a Roman soldier carries on his back a tightly gathered bundle of straight rods. It seems an odd thing for anyone to be carrying, let alone a soldier. I recognized this strange object as a *fascio* (pronounced 'fasheeo'), which was a well-known symbol of Roman power at the time of Jesus. The *fascio* illustrates that one stick can easily be broken but many sticks, bound together tightly, are much stronger. In the nineteenth and twentieth centuries the *fascio* became the symbol of the fascist movement, inspired by the Roman Empire's ability to bring about unity through strength and strength through unity.

For fascists, power comes through submitting the individual will to the national 'good'. Uniformity and obedience are practical virtues for the fascist which lead to efficiency and prosperity for all who submit and conform. This way of thinking exists to this day among many uniformed institutions, but most especially the military. Characteristics of fascism, a tendency towards uniformity and control, can be seen at different times and places in many institutions, military, civil and religious. Religions that demand ethical and creedal orthodoxy exhibit this type of crushing tidiness and orderliness which demeans humanity as much as it aims to nurture it. If we see fascist unity in our community of faith, we do well to resist and walk away. The statues of Jesus and the Roman soldier, side by side, in Lourdes, reminded me of the contrast between fascism and true religion. The statue of Jesus was illustrative of a broken stick that refused to be bound to the imperial power of Rome; the solider by his side with the rest of the bundle of straight rods slung on his back gazes up at the rod that would not stay straight but chose brokenness instead. In that brokenness Jesus sought unity with all those who are broken by the *fasci* of tyrants.

In contrast to fascist unity there is authentic religious community. The word 'religion' has its roots in the Latin word *ligio*. In English this can be translated as 'binding'. *Ligio* is also where we get the English word 'ligament', that thin sinew that binds our bones together allowing us to move with suppleness and freedom. Without the ligaments to bind our muscles to our bones, most of our muscles would be useless. A muscle and a bone, far from losing their autonomy, become animated and empowered by their connection; their freedom is defined by their relationship. Modernity and capitalism have given us a narrow understanding of freedom as the ability of the individual to act out and express their individuality unhindered by the state and society. Far better is the anarchist conception of freedom: freedom of association and mutual aid. In this definition the individuated self is free to associate with whoever they choose. While it is true that some associations may become unhealthy, by and large, the greater the commitment we have to one another the greater our personal freedoms to act and express our widest aspirations.

Saul Alinsky, an early pioneer of community organizing in Chicago in the 1930s, defines power simply as the ability to act. Wherever there is the potential for a person or people to act, there is the possibility that others will be acted upon. Sometimes to act on someone is benign: a surgeon removing a tumour from her patient or a parent restraining his child on the bus.

Sometimes to act on others causes harm: physical and emotional abuse, corporations polluting environments. Every day we act on one another and most of the time it is welcomed implicitly but often there remains a tension between good and bad, or welcome and unwelcome power. When spiritual activists are willing to be religious members mutual flourishing, greater freedom and power to bring about change follow.

The opposite extreme to fascism is structurelessness. Both in the Church and in various leaderless grassroots groups I have met people who are so opposed to leadership that they create a tyranny of a more subtle kind. People set up teams, programmes and events and then refuse to take explicit responsibility for leading them. The result is that new people do not feel welcome, regular members feel let down and confused, and decisions are made without accountability or agreement. If action is taking place, then power can be assumed in its being used. This is a neutral fact. How that power is being used is never a neutral fact and should always be open to scrutiny.

Broadly speaking there are two kinds of power. Both are morally neutral and can be used for good or ill. There is 'power over' or positional power. This is the kind of power that acts on the basis of authority that is either voluntarily handed over or taken by force. Sometimes positional power is used to mutual benefit and sometimes exploitatively. Then there is 'power with' or relational power. This second kind of power is built when people commit to each other as relational human beings with a long-term commitment to each other's wellbeing. Relational power is built when people are valued ahead of projects and plans. In religion we find both, but, at its best, it offers an example of relational power that can bring about a greater common good. Of course, religion is rarely at its best. But then again, whatever is? An enchanted activist cannot be a lone ranger but must live with others in a deeply committed way and be willing to do the soul work of listening, negotiating and being acted on by a community. We must be reacquainted with the rich gift and ambiguity of power in order to be enchanted in our activism. Power is neither good nor bad but simply the means by which things get done and yet we must always be suspicious of its use, especially when power is unaccountable or hidden.

In Mansfield, Nottinghamshire, I helped set up a local alliance of civic institutions called Maun Valley Citizens. Through this alliance we have been learning about the power of building relationships through one-to-one sharing of our stories. And the geography itself helps generate these stories. The river Maun lends its name to our alliance and passes through the post-industrial towns of Ashfield and Mansfield. Back in day these were prospering communities surrounded by pit-villages and built on the wealth of coal mining, shoe and hosiery manufacturing and thriving markets. At one point there were a dozen mills in and around

Mansfield where yarn was spun and shipped out around the country and beyond. All that is gone now, and although the warmth of welcome for strangers is still vital to the area's character, civic society is also not what it once was. We stopped weaving civic society when we stopped weaving.

Intrigued by the weaving history of our town I bought a drop spindle. A drop spindle is a simple-looking device made from a piece of doweling and a wooden disc with a small hook on one end. It's used to tease out a skein of sheep's wool into a yarn for weaving or knitting. The spindle is a spinning weight that pulls the wool downwards as it twists until it becomes a yarn. You have to slowly tease it out with the skein over your shoulder and the spindle dangling and twisting in one hand while the other hand coaxes the wool down and together. Spinning in this way is a conversation between a simple wooden tool and a chaotic jumble of fleece that results in a strong and versatile yarn. A yarn, helpfully, being another word for a story exactly because we spin out stories just as we spin out yarns of wool.

This is the essence of the one-to-one conversation. Several members of St Mark's Church, where I was based, trained in organizing and campaigning, and two people volunteered to be at the back of church at the end of our principal service each Sunday for four weeks to tease out the stories from our members. A small team also went to the homelessness project called The Beacon, run by another member church, to have one-to-one conversations there too. It was in the cafe there that we kept hearing stories about a particular housing provider called Haven Homes. Haven Homes were receiving both a rental income and state money to support vulnerably housed people plus an extra maintenance fee taken from the tenants. We heard stories of shockingly poor standards of accommodation with damp walls, badly fitting windows, over-charging for repairs and illegal opening of residents' post. One young pregnant woman told us that the landlord had come into her property and cut off her fridge and oven because they were unsafe but provided no support to get another. A former resident told us that after a resident killed himself in one of the flats, the blood was not cleaned from the wall or the mattress before a new tenant was moved in. When the new tenant complained, he was told to turn the mattress over.

As a local alliance of schools and faith groups we felt that a formal investigation was needed. Since mayoral elections were around the corner, we asked the candidates for mayor to commit, if elected, to undertake an investigation. And to push our message home we carried out two public actions. The first action was an assembly of over 300 people to hold the public officials to account in holding the inquiry. The second action took place after the mayoral elections: 60 people from seven churches gathered together and invited the newly elected mayor to update us on her progress with the inquiry. We then marched on the offices of Haven Homes, dressed in white boiler suits and carrying a banner that read 'Haven Homes is Toxic'. To our surprise, many of the residents came out of the office as we arrived, shouting and swearing at us and telling us we should not be making them homeless. We later learnt that staff had told them to say this. We noticed a minibus parked nearby and the Director standing in the office window watching the drama unfold, but he was to be disappointed. Many churches hold to the ancient religious ritual of 'sharing the peace'. Since Haven Homes needed to be a real haven of peace, I used that ritual right there. I stood on a traffic island nearby and addressed both sets of protestors, asking for a minute of respectful silence. To my surprise this happened immediately. Then, having explained the difference between the pacification of bullying landlords and the real peace of God, which is wholeness and healing, I invited our alliance to 'share the peace'. This was unrehearsed and yet immediately they turned to each other with hugs and handshakes saying, 'Peace be with you.' They then turned to the counter-protestors and offered the same. Most of the tenants accepted the offer of peace. Two women hugged each other close; although on opposite sides of this protest, they knew each other from The Beacon project. As they hugged, the resident of Haven Homes whispered, 'I'm sorry, I don't even know why I'm here!'

Later they told us more of their story. They said they had been bribed with cider and cash and had been told we wanted to close down Haven Homes and make them street homeless. Since then we have continued to work with the Mayor and with residents of Haven Homes to ensure each house in our area receives a proper inspection, with fines imposed where necessary and changes made. In the Bible, the prophet Isaiah said that God would give the disposed people a 'garment of praise instead of a spirit of mourning'. By teasing out the yarns and then weaving them together we have seen this miracle in action in our own time.

Change comes about when we bring together diverse people who would not normally meet and allow them space to share their stories. This mix is explosive, dynamic and world-changing. I did not learn a lot in chemistry lessons at secondary school, but I do remember the more explosive elements. Potassium is a metal that is as soft as butter and highly reactive, and it fizzes and explodes into potassium hydroxide when dropped into water. We were wide-eyed. We had managed to sneak away some magnesium the week before and hoped that if we got hold of enough potassium we might be able to blow up one of the school toilets. Fortunately for all concerned we never got close. But I learnt that water is boring on its own, and potassium is only a bit more interesting on its own, but you only need to get these two diverse substances together and not only do things really heat up and get exciting but you end up with an entirely new thing: potassium hydroxide and a release of hydrogen gas.

Bringing together diverse elements is a fundamental wisdom of healthy ecosystems – whether it's companion-planting onions with carrots to ward off carrot fly, or whether it is creating meandering borders of contrasting environments to generate greater health and abundance – diversity always generates interactions and dynamism. Socially this is also true. I have spent enough time in ideologically sectarian subcultures to know that they are mentally tyrannous and emotionally uninspiring. Above all they do not change anything. The reason purist political groups do not change the world is because they fail to communicate and negotiate with it. I am proud to have been a member of an Inclusive Church and to be part of the Inclusive Church network. This is a network of churches that 'does not discriminate, on any level, on grounds of economic power, gender, mental health, physical ability, race or sexuality'.[18] But more than that, our church includes people who read liberal left-wing newspapers, reactionary right-wing ones and everything between. We have pacifists, and we have people who support the military. We have vegans and fast-food fans. This means we have to talk *to* each other instead of *about* each other. It is exciting and always leads to new compounds, new material and the building of a new common good. One of the reasons some activists become disenchanted is because they allow their activism to be ghettoized, blaming the outsider for not 'getting it'. Religious communities gather people not on the basis of their strength but rather on the honest reality of our human frailty.

In the summer of 2001, I was sitting in the sun-soaked backyard of perhaps the most expensive squatted building I had ever been in. It was a London property, valued at over £4 million, which was being unofficially looked after by an anarchist collective who had opened up several of the rooms for community use. Here we sat sipping herbal teas and smoking rollies while debating and analysing the broken politics that left people hungry and homeless. The conversation was stimulating, angry and passionate. Yet somehow I left disappointed. We had moved on a little but had mostly rehearsed our ideals without finding any solutions. We lacked a language of myth and purpose.

There is no proof that all humans are spiritual and want a collective expression of their spirituality, but expressing our aspirations and mysteries collectively has a dynamic effect on both the individual and the group. Corporate spiritual practice allows us space to work imaginatively at the social justice problems that we face. It also gives us an opportunity to see ourselves in the whole and the whole in ourselves as we get way from the reductionist tendencies of modern life and allow the complexity of the human experience to be something beyond the material experience. To be an activist who has religion is to be a person with a ready-made community of both inspiration and frustration that grounds us in the diverse reality of being a human. As an activist who was also a parish priest I found this tension hugely helpful and healthy. I could break into an RAF base one day and be in conversation with a member of the congregation, with family in the RAF, the next day. The space in between us is where truth lies. Far from being a place where everyone is coerced into pretending to agree with each other, healthy religion is a place where diverse people can disagree well and go beyond ideology and moral purity to a place of understanding and joint venture. People are enchanting. But religion so often comes at a cost and often that cost is too high. A couple who lived with us at the vicarage, who were in a same-sex relationship, were told by the institutional church that their love was inferior. One of them felt called to be a priest but was told she had to choose between marriage and ordination. She chose love over piety, and they are now part of a Quaker church where they are welcomed more fully as who they are. It is better to walk away rather than put up with abuse, neglect or physical harm.

Many people, all over the world, have heard of Mahatma Gandhi, a founding father of the Indian nation. But in India the figure of Bhimrao Ambedkar is just as famous, particularly among the Dalits. The Dalits used to be known by all kinds of pejorative names: untouchable, outcaste, Harijan (a euphemism for illegitimacy), to name a few. But for Dalit activists the term 'Dalit' has become a signifier of defiance. It means 'of the soil' but also 'crushed'. Ambedkar was a Dalit leader during the twentieth century who, like Gandhi, was a founder of the nation.

Ambedkar was brought up as a Hindu in a poor family but managed to become a lawyer, and in the process he became an incredible activist. Even today, many Dalits are considered Hindu, although their customs and beliefs pre-date Hinduism and, crucially, they are still informally barred from entry into many Hindu temples, because they are considered unclean. Furthermore, the traditions and texts of Hinduism were used to marginalize and exploit them. In the Manusmriti, for example, the advice is to pour hot metal into the ears of any Dalit who heard the scriptures read out loud. It was against this backdrop of physical and ideological violence that Ambedkar led hundreds of thousands of Dalits in a mass conversion from Hinduism to Buddhism. Ambedkar recognized that it was time for him and his neighbours not to reform and refunction Hinduism but to recognize it was never theirs in the first place.

Religion need not be global and institutional, although some activists find their home in more established expressions of spirituality. Religion is simply the contracted community of spiritual seekers who choose to be accountable to one another in forming the sort of spiritual habits that lead to mystical experience and re-enchant us with our broken world. A dozen people, with no creed or liturgy, can do this as legitimately as millions of subscribers to an ancient practice. The key to enchanted religion is our willingness to find freedom and power in our spiritual journeying with others so that we may act.

6

Enchanted by Affliction

Siddhartha Gautama, the prince who became the Buddha, was brought up as a bubble-wrapped prince with a high wall built around his experience of the world. His royal parents were intent on making sure that their young son avoided affliction, because a prophecy at his birth warned that he might become a spiritual teacher instead of a ruler if he ever experienced suffering. Like all parents of teenagers who try to protect their darlings from reality, these parents failed. Prince Siddhartha sneaked out four times, and each time he saw a different aspect of human suffering – poverty, sickness, old age and death – and these pierced him to his soul. Siddhartha abandoned his privileged life and worldly goods and joined a wandering band of ascetics. In an attempt to understand suffering, Siddhartha experimented in increasingly extreme self-denial. Reaching the brink of starvation and death, he was rescued by a passing girl who nursed him back to life. Restored to health, he realized that extreme suffering would not enlighten him any more than extreme wealth would bring him happiness. He chose a middle way and began his successful journey towards true enlightenment. This is a founding story of Buddhism, illustrating eternal truths about the human condition. We cannot change the world by purging our lives, waiting until we are completely pure and unworldly before we discover truth. Truth is not found in pain, humiliation or abstention but rather in genuine solidarity with those who are afflicted. The Buddha discovered that the heart of affliction is the universal desire to be free from suffering. Freedom from the desire to be free from suffering is an ever deeper understanding of affliction.

When I was a teenager at school, I once ran into a toilet door at great speed. By mistake. I can't remember if I was running after someone or away from someone, but I do remember that it hurt. My vision blurred, and a little while later I became dizzy and nauseous, suffering with concussion. My mum was called in, and I was taken to hospital. I remember opening the car door as we drove across the suspension bridge that separated our island from the mainland where the hospital was – about 200 metres up – it must have frightened the life out of my mum. I am told I spoke fluent Welsh to the nurse. This was the first and only time I ever managed to do so. Few of us choose pain, and for good reason, even if it means we can speak Welsh.

Simone Weil

The pain of running into things, or getting a toothache for a bit, or missing lunch: these are physical upsets that demonstrate attachment to the desire to avoid suffering. This is pain, not affliction, although they are often connected. Affliction is a word much used by the French mystic Simone Weil to describe something far deeper than pain but that is sometimes linked to it. We are afflicted when we experience a pain that begins the process of destroying the self. Affliction is not pain, but neither is it despair either. Despair is a reaction to affliction we do not come to terms with and make use of. Despair can be a comfort blanket in a world of affliction. With this in mind we might think that affliction is a terrible thing but Simone Weil argues that affliction is not bad, but is more ambiguous than that. Weil describes affliction as the wall of the cell in which we find ourselves separated from God. Although the wall separates us from God it is also the only means by which we may communicate with God, through the vibrations that this barrier creates. Affliction, which is inevitable, can be harnessed as a means of discovering true mystical experience among the illusions and idols of everyday life…if we let it. We may experience affliction because of our own suffering, we might also experience affliction because we have deeply connected to the suffering or affliction experienced by other people or by nature. The latter is a mystical experience of affliction that connects us not with our humanity or our inhumanity but rather our spirituality: that which is beyond self and is united with all things. This is where we experience what is on the other side of Simone Weil's allegorical cell wall. By attending to our own affliction and by finding spiritual practices that lead us down a mystical pathway to the affliction of others, we experience that union with all things that is itself divine and enchanting.

The practical means of enchanted affliction is symbolic and practical compassion. Compassion is a deliberate and purposeful coming alongside those who are afflicted, either symbolically or in total surrender to their affliction. The word 'passion' means to suffer affliction. People who are in love are often called passionate because they suffer with longing for the object of their affections, the subject of poems and ballads. In the Christian tradition passion refers to the isolation, torture, death and execution of Jesus of Nazareth. The days leading up to commemorating Jesus' crucifixion are called 'Passiontide' and worshippers remember his passion, or suffering, through liturgies, dramas, pilgrimages and scriptural readings. This is a much stronger and more literal use of the word 'passion' than romantic love and an exemplary of enchanted affliction.

Here are two ways of expressing compassion, although they might be seen as a continuum. Broadly speaking there are symbolic and vicarious acts of compassion. Symbolic compassion is a way of participating in the affliction of others through meaningful gesture. Just as words are symbols so too are actions. Sometimes we use symbols to communicate with others. Sometimes we use symbols to communicate only to ourselves. In symbolic compassion we communicate our intention and longing to connect with the affliction experienced by others to understand it and so do something to lift or share that affliction. Pilgrimage, fasting or a sponsored run on behalf of a loved one can all be made examples of symbolic affliction.

There is nothing wrong with a moderate amount of symbolic travel along the road of affliction. But if this self-denial is for self-realization, or if it replaces concrete political solidarity, it is self-defeating. Activists will often face spells in jail or prison for the sake of a cause, knowing that their suffering is just an echo of the affliction of the people they mean to support. Sometimes it may embody their own affliction as politically alienated or socially marginalized people. I sat in a police cell for nearly two days while my house was raided by police after a non-violent direct action in solidarity with children in Afghanistan who are afraid to sleep at night for fear of British drone warfare. But my experience of symbolic compassion was nothing but a faint arrow pointing to their very real affliction. A child in an Afghan village knows experientially that the droning noise above their head often means another civilian family will die tonight. That family might be their own. This fear pierces the child's soul and slowly destroys the self. I cannot replicate this in an airfield in Lincolnshire and would not choose to do so even if I could. But when I take my experience of political solidarity and use it as an opportunity for contemplation, for non-verbal prayer, I may be drawn closer to the affliction of the child in Afghanistan; perhaps close enough to feel the edge of the shadow of that fear and horror and know that it degrades the dignity of us all. With symbolic compassion we make an offering to the divine as we wrestle for a new spiritual and temporal reality.

If symbolic compassion is an offering then vicarious compassion can be said to be a sacrifice. As the enchanted activist Phil Berrigan (1923–2002) put it, 'If they come for the innocent, without stepping over your body, cursed be your religion and your life.' Sometimes it is necessary, possible and useful to step in and put our bodies in the way of harm.

Vicarious compassion takes us further than symbolic compassion. To suffer vicariously is to take the place of another, to stand where they were meant to stand so that they do not have to stand there. This is what martyrs do when they choose a path they know will lead to death. They challenge the systems that afflict others. This is why the death of a soldier in conflict is a tragedy and but not an act of martyrdom. The soldier knows death is possible but does their best to avoid it and would choose the death of a stranger, who they call enemy, sooner than their own. This is not 'the ultimate sacrifice' as it is often

referenced in British culture, since it is never chosen.
The exemplar of vicarious compassion is the Jesus of
the gospel writers' story. Jesus was neither particularly
poor nor wealthy but experienced the affliction of
occupation by the Romans, and a leadership that had
become compromised. To begin with, his campaign
of symbolic radical compassion connected him deeply
with the affliction of both his fellow oppressed Jews
and the Jewish and foreign agents of oppression. These
connections enabled him to go beyond the 'us and
them' of most solutions. This ability to live as one who
recognizes oneness in affliction made him a threat to
the status quo. He was arrested, brutalized and killed.
According to accounts, Jesus believed that at any point
he could have stopped this from happening by calling
on angels to intervene, he could have defended himself
against his accusers and escaped the wrath of the Roman
Empire. But Jesus faced crucifixion instead. And in
his moment of death his self-identification with the
affliction of others was so great that witnesses record
him as having called out, 'My God, my God, why have
you forsaken me?' just before he died. That sense of the
utter forsakenness of self is at the outer limits of affliction
and the point beyond which there is only death and
resurrection. But the word 'resurrection' does not fully
encompass what happens when we get to the end of the
journey of vicarious compassion and come out the other
side. What comes out the other side of the tomb is not

the old self, but rather it is the cosmic human who has completely been drawn into the affliction of the other, found God and the nadir of existence and come back fully united with all things. This is what is so enchanting about affliction.

We skirt the edges of deep magic when we act symbolically in solidarity with those who are oppressed, but we dive in and drown in it when we fully give ourselves vicariously to the affliction of the other. Compassion is, perhaps, beginning to sound noble and desirable. Why is it then that we so often talk about 'compassion fatigue'? The compassion we offer so often feels unsustainable and we easily become disenchanted and choose not to feel too deeply the affliction of others in case we burn out. When we allow our compassion to become romantic, relentless and impotent in the face of overwhelming injustice, it is easy to become disillusioned and despairing. When we become disenchanted with affliction we cease to act.

We are romantic in our compassion in as much as we imagine those who are afflicted abstractly rather than actually getting to know them. When we know people we are not only moved by their sadness but also by their character and their joys. The romanticized Oppressed Other is an endless cry of affliction that eventually stops us from hearing the real and complex humanity of real and lived experience. It is the stuff of nightmares, not the stuff of life. For 12 months an activist friend of mine called Penny organized monthly vigils outside RAF Waddington, where UK drones are piloted from. This was not a romantic solidarity with exotic strangers. At these vigils there would be a live internet conversation with activists in Afghanistan, many of whom were known personally to people at the vigil and who, as part of the group Voices for Creative Non-violence UK, had made friends with Afghans in the UK and in Afghanistan. The people of whom we spoke were not tragic stills in out-of-date newspapers. They were survivors and human beings with their own agency and complex reality.

It is not only the totality of the problem that can overwhelm us but also the relentlessness of individual examples of brokenness that many of us meet on an almost daily basis and feel unable to help. A couple of years ago, just as autumn was turning wintry, a man came to the door, who was street homeless. I was living in a vicarage, so this is nothing new, although not a daily happening. The man was in his late sixties and went by the name of Rocky. He was drunk and remained so for the three days I knew him. When he spoke, he was hard to understand and did his best to avoid answering any questions. I got Rocky a cup of sugary coffee and a cheese sandwich, phoned a local homeless charity and handed over the phone. Rocky had lung cancer and had discharged himself from hospital. He was clearly sick. We arranged a taxi to get him back to the hospital, but he disappeared before it arrived only to reappear later. At night he slept in the porch of the church hall, shouting at the shadows in his sleep. Three times each day he came to my door for food and drink and conversation, including a conversation where I tried to explain why taking apart our garden path was not useful, even if it was badly put together, and he used to be a builder. On day three Rocky came to the door when I was out and made loud threats to a woman who was staying with us. I explained to him the next morning that he must visit the charity down the road to get onto the housing list. If he did, he could come back for another coffee and sandwich. We never saw Rocky again. It seems unlikely that he lived much longer.

Throughout the time Rocky was with us, one of Jesus' parables hung over my head like an ominous cloud. It was the parable of the poor man sitting at the gate of the rich man's house. In this story both men died and the poor man, Lazarus, goes to the bosom of Abraham while the rich man, unnamed, goes to the flames of hell. Still thinking himself entitled to be served by others, the rich man asked Abraham to send Lazarus to him with water to help ease his torment. Abraham claimed that this was impossible since a great chasm had been fixed between them. Still failing to recognize Lazarus' humanity, the rich man asked Abraham to send him to his wealthy brothers to warn them. Rocky and I had looked at each other from across that great chasm and it was in that encounter that I realized that the chasm between the rich and the poor is not fixed in the next life by God but in this life by us. Most of the time, I ignore the breach. Only when I try to reach across it, to soothe myself while further dehumanizing those who society has left vulnerable, do I see how wide the gap really is. In encounters like this we can easily believe ourselves to be experiencing 'compassion fatigue' and in need of a break from our heroic marathon of service to others. What we are really experiencing is the horror of our own complicity. What we really need is to repent and be baptized in the affliction of others: the practice of compassion.

Fasting as symbolic compassion

In 2014, I fasted for 40 days. I drank fruit juice each morning and the water left over from when my family had steamed vegetables. Otherwise it was water only for five and a half weeks. This was fasting as symbolic compassion. We were seeing an increasing number of people dependent on food aid in the UK – perhaps 500,000 or more. That number went on to double in the following year, as reports by Trussell Trust and by an All Party Parliamentary Group attested as well as numerous academic and charity reports and papers. At the time, a substantial majority of these people were under benefit sanctions, waiting for benefits to be processed, or in some other crisis related to low-paid insecure work and the escalating cost of food (up 30.5% in the previous five years). Increasing numbers of people were one unexpected bill away from bare cupboards. Our population was less than 70 million, but we had 10 million people in poverty and 3.5 million of those were children. The majority of households in poverty were working households. Sixty per cent of families with an income under £17,000 had to cut back on food spending, with parents missing meals to feed their children. I have written all this in the past tense, because it describes the state in which we found ourselves in 2014.[19] A new Conservative government bailed out banks while clobbering the poorest with benefit caps and sanctions, like never experienced since the welfare state was developed. Arguably, the situation at the time of writing is far worse, with both increased poverty and a private debt burden of around £70 billion as people dug into their savings and beyond to meet the rising cost of living with a lower income.[20] At the time that this crisis was unfolding, I was a parish priest and activist in Mansfield, a former mining and textiles town in Nottinghamshire. This town had prospered during the industrial revolution and beyond. When the pits, factories and train lines were all shut down in the 1980s, the town lost its economic vibrancy but somehow not its courage. The well-paid and secure work was replaced by insecure contracts, low-skilled and low-paid work. When the government's 'austerity' experiment hit the town of Mansfield, it hit hard. Three foodbanks were set up to meet the rising challenge of hunger in the town. These sat alongside other voluntary groups that fed and clothed the growing number of homeless and vulnerably housed people around us. Since then one of the largest regional charities working with homeless people has lost nearly all its funding and has pulled out of the town. Another charity, working with homeless people from prison, has also lost all funding for this work.

One of my most poignant experiences of this epidemic of poverty happened on Christmas Eve in 2013. Vivian, a homeless woman whom my family had got to know and who had been to our house for tea and a chat occasionally, came to us to say that the flat she had been staying in had no gas or electricity. The tenant, her partner, had no money to pay the rent for the electricity meter. Her welfare payments had been used to pay off some of his debts, and she had no food. Occasionally, we would find people in our garden at night, or evidence they had slept rough the next morning. Always their experiences of life had left them in a vulnerable state, even if they presented as aggressive and loud. It seemed ludicrous to me that in one of the richest nations in the world an increasing number of people could live so precariously. Five minutes' walk from her flat were houses worth half a million pounds. Living in a large vicarage we usually had someone staying in our spare room, housing up to four people at a time with us, although we had breaks in between guests, for us to just be a small family again. The people who shared our lives so intimately reminded us of how precarious human flourishing is when it can disappear with structural injustice and a few bad choices. I was connected to colleagues around the country who helped run or set up foodbanks, soup kitchens and community cafes. They were seeing all the same signs of crisis that I was and their churches were responding by urgently meeting the needs of people in crisis. Like me they felt uncomfortable with this reactive response to the breakdown of the welfare state's safety net. Those who came to foodbanks felt the shame and stigma of it, however friendly and compassionate the volunteers there might be. The volunteers knew that, however many people they helped, there would be others who were hidden in their hardship. We felt like steam valves for an unjust system when really we wanted to be whistle-blowers, so that the system's failures might be exposed. In parliament, politicians were openly celebrating the growing number of foodbanks as a sign of a healthy society. Laughing at stories of hardship and humiliation, they claimed credit for stimulating compassion by creating scarcity for the masses even while the rich got even richer. And at the more fascist end of our media editorials had gone from demonizing people for receiving state handouts to vilifying those who used foodbanks too. They claimed that people who used foodbanks were probably faking and were too lazy to work or too ignorant to cook. They had returned us to the Victorian narrative of poverty as a symptom of moral failure. It was in this context that I got a phone call from a friend, George Gabriel, who is a community organizer and deeply compassionate agitator, also angry but determined to be proactive in his response to the malaise of government.

Together with a small team of talented, committed and relationally minded activists we created a national campaign called End Hunger Fast. Our core team really was fewer than half a dozen people, spread across the country, who met via the internet each week and in person when we could. We had a good spread of skills including organizing, press work, fundraising, research, web development, public engagement, creative and theological reflection and administration. Rather than say what we wanted and then find the people, we first found the passionate people and then worked out what we could do together. George built a team and organized it to build the action. Beyond that we built strong partnerships with key national leaders and national charities, identifying where we had shared interests and negotiating outcomes and strategies along the way. For me this was a steep learning curve. I learnt how a small number of organized people, willing to make personal and financial commitments to each other, can change a national narrative and have fun doing so.

The outline of our campaign was simple. We would launch 40 days of fasting during the Church's season of

Lent in February and March 2014. This would begin with a letter from faith leaders, including as many bishops as were willing, and a commitment from these public leaders to fast for at least one day during the 40 days, in solidarity with those who go hungry. We would also have a national day of fasting. We would have as many people as possible undergoing a total 40-day fast. Just a week before we were due to begin our campaign the Roman Catholic Church hit out at the government over food poverty and the Prime Minister responded defensively.

We needed to launch early and sent out our letter, ahead of schedule, securing a front page exclusive with the *Mirror* newspaper: '27 bishops slam David Cameron's welfare reforms as creating a national crisis in unprecedented attack'.[21] Leaders from various denominations also backed the public letter, and it was followed by letters from rabbis and from over 70 university academics on food policy. Over the course of the campaign, working closely with grassroots and national charities, we continued to raise the issues. We estimated several thousand people fasted with us. We got five national papers to run front pages and double-page spreads. We used interviews on countless regional and national radio programmes and on prime-time news and other TV programmes and got a private meeting with the Prime Minister to challenge him directly. Meanwhile, teams in Birmingham and Leicester set up public fasting vigils at their Anglican cathedrals, and a team in North Wales ran a high-profile local campaign. Rapidly, the culture and language around foodbanks and food poverty began to change. Since then there have been some significant gains as regards better care of those who may be put under welfare sanctions and two serious All-Party Parliamentary Group reports. At the end of the campaign we launched a final letter, this time signed by more than 40 bishops, including one archbishop. A follow-up campaign called 'End Hunger UK' has since developed the ideas as the national charities continue to faithfully empower those whom government would silence.

There was a huge amount of behind-the-scenes work in the months leading up to the campaign and a massive amount of media exposure in the week that it ended. Much of this was in very new contexts for me; most of my experience of the media till then had been fairly local or regional. But for the vast majority of the 40 days itself, I was able to keep my head down and concentrate on the spiritual discipline of fasting that underpinned the campaign. In the end only three of us took part in the 40-day fast, but I was extremely glad of the company. I would not recommend such an extreme action. It is not a healthy thing to do. But if you are going to be fasting for an extended period, then you may as well learn about how I did it as safely as I knew how. There is very little out there written about the practicalities of an extended full fast.

The practice of fasting

Before I got anywhere near my fast, I checked in with my community of faith. I spoke to my spiritual guide, my boss, and some of my church members as well as people of other faiths and of good faith who I knew and who knew me well enough to challenge my actions constructively. I also talked it through with my wife, since this decision would have a considerable impact on her too. Many of these people were offered a veto over my decision. They are people I have chosen to be accountable to. I visited my doctor, explained what I was doing and asked for a basic health check which the doctor was happy to offer, wishing me well with my challenge and offering some observations about the possible effects on my body. Most medical people I spoke to were cautiously supportive or did not oppose the idea outright.

The next step was to look at my diary and see what social and physical hurdles were coming up during the 40-day fast and how many I could manage away and which ones I would have to face. In the ten days prior to the fast I reduced my food portions and cut out grains and all processed food, alcohol and caffeine. This meant that I could deal with the headaches and nausea of coming off these substances before dealing with the hunger. It also allowed my stomach to shrink a little in advance. As a result of this preparation I experienced no hunger pangs when the fast began. In fact, I did not feel any hunger pangs until day 28 of the fast. I did not reduce my intake to absolute zero. I had decided to drink a glass of fruit juice every morning and the water left over from when my family had steamed vegetables each evening. In retrospect I might have not had the juice in the morning as I think the sugar rush was annoying and unnecessary, but the warm mineral-rich water probably kept me alert as did regular cups of mint tea and glasses of cold water throughout the days. Simon Cross, one of the people who fasted with me, managed on only vitamin supplements and water. Scott Albrecht, a Catholic activist, experimented with a daily can of vegetable juice for the first few mornings, with unpleasant consequences. All of us went about our usually daily activities throughout the fast.

More important than the preparation for fasting is how an extended fast is carefully brought to an end. Three of us took part in this 40-day fast. One became extremely ill, because he ate too much too soon. In extreme cases this can lead to permanent damage. It can even be fatal. I broke my fast with a teaspoon of peanut butter. My family and some friends who were staying with us that year sat together with a spoonful each. We sat in our living room and licked peanut butter from our respective spoons. Later I had some nettle soup and pureed pears and then didn't eat anything until the next day. For the next two days I mostly ate baby food from jars as I was rushing around public actions for the end of the campaign. The jars proved extremely useful and tasted good too, although I did not get the full effect of eating baby food, choosing not to spread it all over my face and on the walls as I had when I was an actual baby.

I wonder if going beyond 28 days without food is the point at which extended fasting gets extreme. It was for me. This is one lunar cycle which, for primitive humans, would be the equivalent of a hunting cycle. Lions hunt when the sky is at its darkest so humans would wait for the full moon to go out hunting. For hunter-gatherers life was a series of lunar cycles of feast and famine. When I reached 28 days, I began to crave meat. I would lie awake at night fantasizing about liver and onions or raw steak. Simon and Scott, both vegans, had none of these cravings but did experience a physical and emotional low point at about the same time. I do not know if they lay awake craving cashew nuts and grilled tofu. It took me about a week to shake off this fug: I had begun to count down the days till the end of my fast, in my head, which reawakened my attachment to eating. The breakthrough came on day 35, when I made an act of the will to savour the last week of my fast knowing I was unlikely to do anything like this again, or for a long time.

I learned about attachment and desire through this extended fast. Most of the time not eating was easy. I was not afflicted like people who go hungry through poverty. This was a symbolic act. I had chosen not to eat and knew when I would be able to eat again. My lack of eating was not linked to a complex web of humiliating factors like debt, inability to pay bills, lack of other basic comforts and the indignity of being shamed by others. I never described myself as hungry at any point, and if anyone asked me if I was hungry, I would say, 'No' and do my best to describe what people who were really hungry had told me about their experiences. Another reason I was not hungry was I made the decision, from the very start of the fast, not to desire food. I thought of food as utterly alien to me. I could happily sit with my family while they ate and not feel the slightest pang of attachment to their meals. My youngest did not mention my fast for a week or so, because I would sit at the table just the same as ever. With this daily decision to be non-attached to food I discovered a non-attachment to other desires that began to develop. This was entirely by accident and an unexpected gift. It struck me that perhaps the stomach might be the seat, or anchor, of all other attachments. The nervous system of the stomach acts as a second unconscious mind in the human body which converses with the unconscious brain in our heads. Between them they regulate and influence our physical and emotional wellbeing. To fast is to clear your mind but it is your gut-mind that is being cleared, so that it can teach the head-mind new things. A new sensitivity also developed in me so that I was more ready to empathize with others in their affliction. I have always considered myself a fairly unempathic person but some of this shifted in me during the fast.

Here are some of Simon Cross's early reflections on his fast. You can find more on his blog.

> I woke up this morning with a sense of emptiness in my stomach. Not hunger – the discomfort and craving for food which I experienced in the first few days of my fast are not with me any longer – but a strange hollow feeling. While emptiness is uncomfortable, it is easily bearable. And it is much to be preferred over the early part of the fast, when the body is effectively detoxing and craving all kinds of substances, sugar, salt and fat in particular.
>
> I have now reached the stage of Ketosis, the point in the fast where the body begins to break down its fat deposits via the liver, to turn them into energy. Until this stage ends, I am not expecting to be terribly uncomfortable for a while.
>
> But the thing is this: Most people who are going without food in the UK today are not doing so over long drawn out periods of never eating. They are missing meals here and there, they are going without food for a couple of days at a time.
>
> More than that, they don't have the luxury of planning or researching their hunger, as I have my fast.
>
> Often these short blood sugar draining spells of hunger can lead to rash decisions. Just as most of us know we should not go food shopping when we feel hungry, so it's best not to apply for a pay-day loan while you

have low blood sugar. Hungry people are easy targets for exploitation.

Occasionally rash decisions made when hungry can end up in criminal acts – there is nothing new about this: an ancient Hebrew Proverb calls on God to neither provide too much nor too little – in order that one should neither grow rich and ignore God, or grow poor and have to steal to get what one needs (Proverbs 30.7–9).

Another side effect of the early stages of going without food is a slow down of the body's essential services, in particular the ability to regulate heat. I'm a naturally warm person, but even I was cold and shivery in the first couple of days of the fast.

This reminds me too that one of the big tussles people have financially is with the costs of heating their homes – the ever present card or key meter ticking down until 'clunk' the energy goes off. No central heating, no hot water. The difficult decision of whether to put more money on the gas card, or to get some food is not one to be made when the body is craving sugar.[22]

M.K. Gandhi saw that fasting was a serious spiritual practice that could easily be misused. Gandhi was known for his fasts 'unto death', including one which he may have later regretted when trying to prevent positive discrimination for Dalits in India. One of his less well known and early experiments in fasting is recounted in his biography as a penance on behalf of two of his students who, in his view, had suffered some sort of moral failing. Gandhi fasted for seven days and then ate only one meal a day for four and half months. Gandhi did not see this as a manipulation. In his explanation, he gives us a useful lesson in separating fasting from the practice of a hunger strike.

> Where there is no true love between the teacher and the pupil, where the pupil's delinquency has not touched the very being of the teacher and where the pupil has no respect for the teacher, fasting is out of place and may even be harmful. Though there is thus room for doubting the propriety of fasts in such cases, there is no question about the teacher's responsibility for the errors of his pupils.[23]

Gandhi points to the importance of a clear intention in the fast and one that is founded in compassion and social contract. While a fast may be political it must also be personal and sincere, otherwise it is shallow noise-making. Gandhi fasted when he felt the necessity for symbolic compassion and personal repentance and believed that through this practice he might know God and humanity outside himself and bring the two together for justice and peace. Because justice is right relationships rather than a moral code, fasting is a helpful spiritual practice when the intention is to reconcile people in an oppressive relationship to one another.

Pain is an everyday reality, but to be a disciple of enchanted affliction is to act compassionately in the face of despair. Symbolic affliction can draw the attention of our neighbours to the moral imperative to come together to bring about the inclusion of those who are afflicted: to feed the hungry, clothe the naked, visit those in prison, but also to ask why the people are hungry and naked and what sort of world has to lock away so many of its citizens. Whether affliction is expressed as symbolic or vicarious compassion, it acts primarily on the one who does it. Out of self-transformation the chasm between human beings, in a messed up world, begins to narrow. Fasting is one of many ways in which the enchanted activist might express this radical compassion. We are drawn into the heavenly realm of common affliction because we are all drawn up from the same enchanted earth.

7

Between Heaven and Earth

If you have ever run outside to stand in the rain or fallen about laughing in the mud, you know the joy that comes with breaking down the barriers between our sanitized and civilized lives and the world that we long to be a part of. Cossetted from the harsh realities that the poorest people in our world experience, I have shelter, healthcare and food in the fridge. I am suspended above the earth in my civilized society. Because of this there is something missing: a gap that can only be filled by living by our wits in the natural elements that both frighten and excite us. So often we avoid living our lives with abandon or facing death with grace. We rarely connect with either enough to know who we are and where we belong. Re-enchanting ourselves with the wilderness and with death is a homecoming for us humans. Knowing where we belong we may draw others home.

In a much-loved and well-worn community hall, Billie and I sat down to a turkey and stuffing cob, some crisps and a mug of tea. We had Christmas crackers and a canteen-style fold-away table piled high with every kind of snack food. Around me were a group of other homeless men and women and some friends from our church and neighbourhood, all sharing an early Christmas lunch together. We had decided that this year we were not going to do lunch *for* homeless people. Instead we were going to sit down and have lunch together.

Billie has chosen to spell his name this way, because he believes that in a former life he was a woman who was a warrior. He spells it out to me with a grin on his big bearded face and a twinkle in his eye. He does not care in the least whether I believe his story. He has that painful gift of not holding too tightly to reality. This gift is not one that has helped him negotiate civilization well. In his late teens, Billie tells me, he left home and decided to go feral. With little by way of material resources he set off for the moors and attempted to live off his wits and whatever food he could find. Billie claims to have lived this way for many years, but eventually both his wits and his body ran out of resources. On the point of death by starvation and with a history of violent psychosis, Billie was sectioned and forced to take anti-psychotic injections that he expects to need for the rest of his life. 'I'm alright now, because I've got my injections, but if I miss one then I think everyone wants to kill me, and I want to kill them first,' he says. 'I thought I could do it, but you can't take a domestic animal and set it out in the wild: it'll die or go mad.' Billie should know, if anyone does.

Billie is a reminder of something that most of us rarely notice our whole lives: we are domesticated animals. Our environment has domesticated us. Our evolving genes have domesticated us. Our socializing has tamed our ancient instincts, and even our food has domesticated us. Anthropologists tell us that humans discovered grain around about 10,000 years ago, but it is as true to say that grain discovered humans or perhaps that we found a symbiotic relationship with each other. To maintain its dominant place in nature, grain required humans to settle in towns and clear the land for sowing: it does not like competition and needs bare shocked earth to thrive. In turn grain gives us a mild narcotic high when baked and a relaxing low when brewed. It allowed us to wean our babies younger and therefore have more children. But the price of grain is high: it sucks the marrow out of the earth and demands more and more land or greater chemical and genetic intervention to sustain its monopoly. Grain took us out of the woods and into the city, where we were forced to relate to more people than we ever had before. Pretty soon the sociable, organized humans dominated the nomadic hunter-gatherers, and we began to select our mates on the basis of their ability to negotiate, consolidate and delay or defer violence. We began to domesticate our own genes and have done so with every generation for the last ten millennia.

Fast forward to the twenty-first century with our cavity wall insulation, duvets, antibiotics, sophisticated international relations and sugar- and grain-rich diets, and we see the thick blanket of domestication that has all but hidden our more primitive selves. Journalist and re-wilding campaigner George Monbiot wonders if there is something inherent in us that we long to uncover, something we have lost as housetrained creatures. He points to the odd British phenomenon of people seeing black panthers, where all objective evidence shows that there are none.

Perhaps the imagined beasts lurking in the dark corners of the land reawaken old genetic memories of conflict and survival, memories of encounters – possibly the most challenging our ancestors faced – with large predatory cats. They hint at an unexpressed wish for lives that are wilder and fiercer than those we now lead. Our desires stare back at us, yellow-eyed and snarling, from the thickets of the mind.[24]

Billie is not the only person to 'go feral'. It has been a feature of human self-discovery ever since we first estranged ourselves from the rest of creation. Monbiot points out that in seventeenth- and eighteenth-century North America, elopement of settlers with indigenous people was seen as a real threat to the colonial project. When young men began to abandon Jamestown in

1612, the deputy governor had them hunted down and publicly executed.[25] Adopted by their hosts, it is possible that some of these folk escaped to survive in their more visceral and spiritually animated societies. But Billie's story warns of the shadow-side of this urge to break free from civilization: 'You can't take a domestic animal and set it out in the wild: it'll die or go mad.'

Barefoot

In the Jewish tradition God tells Moses to remove his sandals before approaching holy ground. The earth is described in the Bible's first creation myth in Genesis as 'very good'. The Hebrew word is *tov*, which I think, in this context, should be interpreted as 'voluptuous'. Theology that sits in synod but does not walk our streets is thin gruel. We cannot explore the goodness of the earth without connecting, spiritually, with it.

I was due to speak at a three-day conference on practical theology. I decided to go to the conference barefoot and just see what might happen.

As I stepped on the grass verge at a nearby shopping centre the connection between my carbon-based foot and the grass and soil beneath it became a prayer for a member of my congregation who had died the night before. 'Remember that you are but dust and to dust you shall return.' To get from Mansfield to Cardiff for the conference I needed to walk from my home to the station and then take three trains and a bus. My first challenge was gravel – ouch! I also noticed that the ground was not as dirty and dangerous as I had imagined. I was not constantly avoiding broken glass or other nasties. I noticed my feelings too: self-conscious, vain feelings made me doubt whether I should even be doing this experiment at all. I longed for someone at the station platform to ask me about it so I could explain but no one did so I dealt privately with the possibility of their secret judgements. It gently rained, and I saw that there was nowhere earthy for the rain to go to. It could land on train tracks, concrete, steel and plastic. It could drip down coats and umbrellas. But it could not immediately go home to the earth, as it properly should. The closest material to earth in the area was my feet. They were the closest thing to home for a raindrop on that platform. I thought about the earth as my home and how far beneath my feet it was: beneath the layers of synthetic industrial material was the ground I should be feeling but could not. I was far from 'home', far from the earth to which I belonged both in time and place. My barefoot journey became a lament.

The Right Reverend David Walker has worn only sandals for over 30 years. I met him (and his cat) later that year, and we spoke about his spiritual practice of not wearing socks and shoes:

> It serves as a regular reminder that we are of the earth. Every time I look down and see my feet it is a reminder that we are called to walk gently upon the earth and we

are of the earth and it acts against self-importance and pomposity. There's a huge danger – it's there in spades as a bishop – that one gets such a belief in the sense of one's own importance. Even if I'm at a fancy event, even if I'm talking to senior politicians, government ministers, archbishops, very highly paid business people I am still me: David, a child of God. I might have to wear fancy robes or a dinner jacket but actually that cannot take away my core identity and I must not let it.

Years ago, when I knew that I was going to be a bishop, but it wasn't public, my then-therapist said to me, 'David I've known lots of people become bishops and deans over the years; none of them remained their true self.' That was an excellent little gift for her to give me to take on my journey. With all the stuff that I get pushed and prodded into being, how do I remain 'me'? And the sandals are a visible call to that authenticity, to be the real 'me' in some pretty wild and wacky situation that I inevitably get drawn into.

Activism and mysticism become automatic companions when we have a spirituality that is not simply words and ideas but is embodied. The human body, conscious and sentient, when properly attuned with a deep ecological spirituality is a nerve ending for the earth's pleasure and pain. When a human body experiences a cut, a sore or a rash, then the nerve endings send out a signal so that something can be done. We have become insensitive to the earth's pain and have ceased to be its nerve endings. I have met leprosy victims who have lost limbs due to the damage that the disease causes to their nerve endings: they fail to notice injuries and infections and their extremities – fingers, toes or whole limbs – are eroded. It is an act of transformation and subversion to meditate on the pain of creation. To take off our shoes and enjoy the pleasures of moss and the suffocation of concrete reawakens our commitment to signalling this pain to others. When we do this, we begin to articulate a sense of ecological injustice and do so while not getting dismal by connecting to the joy of the earth. For me, though, above all, barefoot walking was a contemplation of decay, mortality and the cycles of life. It was an awakening to the ever-present gift of death.

Living with death

Death is, or at least it should be, an enchanting partner to life. We brush with death constantly: from our birth we meet invisible bacteria that are born and die in an instant. Our own bodies house a complex society of cells that break down or regrow. We wake each morning enveloped and consumed by a community that is constantly dying and renewing symbiotically with us. We shed dead cells and build new ones on our outsides and insides. Old cells are usually consumed or taken apart and recycled and reclaimed. All this happens without our permission or thanks: a million sacrificial non-human deaths are made in every moment. These deaths keep us alive. We are wise to be grateful and humbled by this. Inside our gut is a whole community of bacteria with no time for mourning but with a heady pace of death to contend with as it transforms both our food and our genes. Whether we are vegans or omnivores, our diet is only possible through the deaths of others. The strictest adherents to the Jain religion cover their mouths in case they ingest a fly and gently sweep before every step in case they tread on an ant. But even they cannot deny complicity with the many deaths that keep them alive. The smell of our skin is generated by cells giving up the ghost and bacteria feasting on dead matter. The intimate and stimulating aroma of the person who holds us close as babies is the smell of death. We notice death when it takes place on a human scale and think of it as something that takes people away from us.

If death is something we think of as a thief who steals from our lives those we love then we are not going to have the best of relationships with it. The feeling of loss is a terrible thing; suffering is awful and the process of dying can be cruel, unnatural and untimely. In wealthier countries we are fortunate that most people live long lives and die peacefully. But this means death is more of a shock, and we are less proficient at engaging with it. The result is that most people want a short, formal and professionalized mourning that allows them to 'move on' without overly dwelling on their own mortality out loud.

But death is as certain and universal as life, and the West has got better at engaging with the human experience of dying in recent decades, particularly with the birth of the hospice movement. In 1947 British nurse Cicely Saunders (1918–2005) came up with the idea of a home for people who are terminally ill, although St Christopher's in South East London only realized this ambition two decades later. Saunders imagined a place dedicated to its patients, with research into methods of holistic care and pre-emptive pain control. While Tibetan Buddhists had known for centuries that accompanying the dying was a very particular skill, in the UK this was cutting-edge thinking. This was the beginning of what we now call the hospice movement, and it has transformed how people in Britain, and in some other countries, engage with the challenges of death and dying. While the West has learnt much from other parts of the world when it comes to care for those who are dying – helping them address their fears, having important conversations with loved ones and confronting their pain – we know little about managing grief and even less about living with death as our partner and constant companion. Benjamin Franklin is famous for saying that 'death and taxes' are the only two certainties in life, although the most powerful seem to avoid the latter, so perhaps now only death has any real certainty about it. Death is the great leveller, which is its gift.

On a research trip to India, I took some time out with my then fiancée Sophie to visit Varanasi, one of the seven holiest cities in India. Varanasi sits on the banks of the holy River Ganges and is, by tradition, the god Shiva's favourite place on earth. The higher steep banks of the Ganges are cluttered with temples of various shapes and sizes. They conceal a maze of the old city's crowded, narrow streets and high-walled houses and hostels. At the edge of the water are the ghats. These are steep steps in neat but rough-hewn stone that warm as the sun rises each day. On our first morning there Sophie and I walked along the ghats a little beyond the chaos to where the steps give way to a narrow and gravelly shore. A small group of people were gathering around a funeral pyre: cedar wood stacked neatly around the body. They poured water and ghee over the pyre, and then a young man stepped forward to set it alight. This took place in full view amidst the ordinary and the everyday, not just the ritual and holy. When all that's left is ashes, these are scattered on the river with prayers for the release of the soul from the cycle of reincarnation into reunion with the divine. We took a wide berth around the funeral and were invited unexpectedly into a tall, run-down red stone building and up some stairs to meet 'the widows of Varanasi'. To be a widow, according to the custom of some, is to be a social and ritual outcaste. These were women who had been discarded by their communities. By some estimates there are nearly 40,000 widows in Varanasi who have been abandoned by their families. They go to this city, where two holy rivers meet, in the hope that by dying here they might be released from reincarnation and go straight to nirvana. Of all the cities in the world few can claim to interweave the themes of life and death as closely as Varanasi. The widows we met were old, but many are young. They asked for a donation to pay for wood for their own funerals. It was brutally stark, honest and pragmatic. The image of these women sitting on the dusty floor next to their piles of wood has stayed with me. Their remaining years were a meditation on their own deaths. As I bathed in the river at dawn the following morning and received the markings of the god Shiva on my forehead, I felt the power and holiness of the place where so many had invested their spiritual hopes and interwoven them with their ordinary lives.

One of the gifts of living in a country like Britain where different faiths rub shoulders is that we can find a challenge to our cultural assumptions among our neighbours. For Muslims the corpse is usually washed and dressed by close family of the same sex, not by a professional to whom we contract out the care for those who have died. If the dead person had performed a pilgrimage to Mecca in their lifetime, then their body is wrapped in the simple white clothes of their pilgrimage. This provides an obvious symbol of death as a pilgrimage begun as well as a journey ended. One cannot wash the body of loved one without being marked by the experience. For West Indian families it is traditional for men to back fill the grave themselves, perhaps singing songs as they work. Any conscious encounter with death changes us, shapes our lives and teaches how to live with death.

Dylan Thomas's most famous poem is a beautiful and passionate rally against dying. It is deeply human and is thought to be a plea not for himself but on behalf of his dying father. It is six angry verses with the regular refrain: 'Do not go gentle into that good night' and 'Rage, rage against the dying of the light'. Rage against the dying of the light? What a miserable and naïve way to experience death. What a cruel and selfish model of dying to wish upon someone we love. But love can be selfish and naïve, when it is not free from attachment and the illusion of eternal personal existence. Perhaps the most banal of all funeral poems is the one written by Anglican priest Henry Scott Holland. He wrote it a century ago, but it remains incredibly popular: 'Death is nothing at all / I have only slipped away into the next room / I am I and you are you / Whatever we were to each other / That we still are…', and so it continues with the same whimsical tripe all the way through, refusing to face up to the hard and dynamic reality of death, even denying grief. In these two poems we hear two extremes of denial of death. On the one hand we treat death as an unnatural opponent to be fought against, on the other we pretend it does not mean anything and that nothing has happened. Both are attempts to avoid the unavoidable.

Although Buddhism describes our mystical relationship to death differently, in many ways Christianity and Buddhism are inviting us to the same re-enchanting of death. Buddhism is well known for the importance it lays on living a life that prepares us for the moment of death. But implicitly both Christianity and Buddhism teach that we are only truly alive – free and fully human – when we live in an appropriate, realistic relationship with death. The Dalai Lama is said to meditate on his moment of death daily, slowing down his breath and his heartbeat to a near standstill until the light of life is almost completely distinguished. This habit is not morbid: it leads to a fuller embrace of life in all its precarious and temporary delight. For many Buddhists, and those they have influenced, the heart of this living in death is the concept of non-attachment. The four noble truths of Buddhism are simply stated but would take many lifetimes to fully explore: all life is suffering; suffering is caused by desire; when we are free from desire (attachment) we are free from suffering; to free ourselves from attachment we must follow the Eightfold Path. The Eightfold Path of Buddhism is a list of ways in which followers of the Buddha attempt to spiritually orientate to be free from attachment. The ultimate attachment is to the illusion of selfhood, as we have already explored. To be free from attachment to self may lead to a re-enchantment with dying and death. Ultimately this may result in a self-emptying, as described by the apostle Paul in his record of a primitive Christian hymn of praise to Jesus quoted in full in Chapter 4. Paul's Jesus 'became completely empty' in order to be in complete solidarity with those who are oppressed. We cannot make the world as it is more just without concrete offers of solidarity, and we cannot be courageous in our solidarity without being willing to self-empty.

Our enchanting journey through life is made easier by understanding the nature and prevalence of death. When death is no longer framed by only human scales of perception but put in context of a universe that is a constantly negotiated exchange between life and death from the cellular level to the stellar scale, then we see death as our ally rather than our stalking enemy.

Recently I was walking with our church youth group through the Peak District in Derbyshire. We passed a graveyard in Edale where the names and all details had worn away from all of the gravestones. Some of our group tried to read some of the names but could not get any sense from them. Being a cheerfully morbid sort I reminded them of the Psalmist's words, 'As for mortals, their days are like grass; they flourish like a flower of the field; for the wind passes over it, and it is gone, and its place knows it no more' (Psalms 103.15–16). These words are not supposed to be an admonishment or an encouragement, they are just a stark reality: whether you're a 'somebody' or a 'nobody' eventually everybody will forget you. It might take a generation, and it might take longer, but it will happen. Whatever you achieve: gone. This equalizing truth allows us to step back from the things we have most invested in and see them as belonging to the community, rather than to us. Humans come and go at a considerable speed. By meditating on our own deaths we allow ourselves a healthy sense of perspective when it comes to risk, loss and gain. Whatever our achievements or failures, we are 'only dust and to dust we shall return'.

During a difficult period in my life several years ago I went through a phase of meditating daily on my own bodily disintegration after death. This practice may seem bizarre but it nourished my soul and returned my joy at a time when nothing else could. I would practise this visual meditation for around 10 to 15 minutes each evening and it was, for a while, the only time when I felt happiness. I still return to this practice occasionally but no longer as a daily habit. You may like to try it. I find that this meditation works best in a dark room, but if you are a more disciplined meditator you might not need that. Remember that no one is in charge of this exercise except you. You decide when it ends.

1. Lie still on a flat surface with your body relaxed.

2. Enter into a deep state of meditative relaxation by focusing on your breath or attending to your body in slow waves of attention from your head down

to your feet. Do whatever helps you to move from your working state to a meditative one.

3. When you are ready, allow your imagination to take you to your own grave, perhaps in a coffin.

4. The grave has already been filled up with the earth that now embraces you all around in the silence of death.

5. Now turn your attention to your gut bacteria: thank them for the work they have done all your life. Tell them – in words if you like – that you have left all external property to others but that you are giving the first fruits of your body to them. At death a process takes place whereby these bacteria that once digested your food turn and begin to digest you. For you the party is over; for them it has just begun.

6. Now imagine all the other stages of decomposition taking place. One need not be too graphic or slow about this but imagine a time-lapse of decomposition as the coffin gently collapses in and you and the soil become one.

7. By the end of this phase of the meditation you are nothing but a barely self-conscious part of the ground that holds the memory of personhood but not the actuality of it.

8. Thank the earth for taking you back and for sending you out into the world for a short while.

9. Spend some time reflecting on the different emotions that come with this feeling of being 'earth to earth'.

10. When you are ready to end this exercise, slowly become aware of your body again. Your toes first, then your feet and ankles and so on. As you become aware again of your body, do so with the same gratitude that has characterized the whole of the meditation.

11. When you have fully returned to the room and to yourself, get up, and go and do something ordinary like drink a glass of water or take a walk.

Death to self

The Christian tradition is abundant in powerful resources to equip us for living with death. The Jesus of Matthew's Gospel described it like this: 'If anyone wishes to come after me, they must deny themselves and take up their cross and follow me' (Matthew 16.24). In case we missed it he immediately adds, 'Whoever wishes to save their life will lose it; but whoever loses their life for my sake will find it.' The metaphor of daily taking up your cross should be a powerful one but even with Jesus' emphasis it can be quickly glossed over. The cross was not a symbol of death but of total annihilation. Spiritual abandonment, social marginalization, and physical torture and death were all tied up in this terrible symbol. People hung on crosses tended to die by suffocation. They would be hung so that they could only breathe by pushing upwards with their legs. Sometimes the Roman authorities would hang thousands of revolutionaries at a time this way; they would be seen like a wave of bodies pushing themselves up and down so that they could gasp for air until, one by one, they became too tired and would collapse, choke and die. Jesus asked the disciples to do this, in a mystical sense, every single day, with the assumption that one day they would have to do this literally; many of them did.

Crucifixion was how the Roman Empire dealt with activists. It was used to cow the masses into submission. Their fear of the suffering that preceded this kind of death – and fear of death itself – kept them from taking the risk of joining together for the common good. By taking up their cross every day, Jesus' followers were choosing not to avoid or romanticize death but to embrace its inevitability and overcome the paralysing fear of it. By dying daily they hoped to be ready, when the time came, to meet with God through death by execution.

A spiritual change from fear and towards enchantment with death develops gradually by habits of spiritual practice. Choices we make in life are influenced by our relationship with death. Paul, who developed much of the early Jesus' tradition and ethics, also developed the theme of living with death. He described the ritual of baptism as a kind of death. This rite, often involving the total immersion in water of the new member of the religious community, was the primary mark of membership, so it was well known to all the communities Paul wrote to. Members of the early Church were expected to live each moment as baptized people, that is, people who are 'dead to sin but alive in Christ Jesus', to quote Paul. For them this language made sense, but it can seem strange to our ears, two thousand years later in other cultures and contexts.

Over the years I have received a fair amount of verbal abuse, and the occasional physical assault, because of activism. The majority of this takes place on the internet, of course. Angry people question my principles, my motives and my integrity. They do not realize that I have long ago come to terms with the fact that my principles are shaky, my motives are mixed and my integrity is a work in progress that I have no hope of completing. They are outing me for something that I already know about myself: I am not good. If I were to look at these comments as though my life had peculiar significance, I might get upset. As it is, I know that life is short and particular. The universe is an ancient, expansive, ever-dynamic mystery. Death to self is a huge comfort in the face of personal attack. If I learn to live daily with death then I learn to give up every attachment. The dead have no reputation to protect and sit lightly to reputation. This is liberating and empowering. Anyone pushing for real change will experience insult and injury from time to time.

On Ash Wednesday, like millions of others, I go to church, and as the priest marks my forehead with the sign of the cross, she prays, 'Remember that you are but dust and to dust you shall return.' These are not words of caution or reprimand but of prayer and liberation. I am invited to live my life in this remembrance. One of the most powerful ways we can connect death to self with social justice is through lamentation. In Jesus' most famous sermon he said, 'Blessed are those who mourn, for they shall be comforted,' but by 'mourn' he meant 'weep, wail and lament', and by 'comforted' he meant, 'see justice done'. At the time of Jesus there were women who daily 'wept for Jerusalem' at the city walls. They mourned the Roman occupation and the tyranny their people were experiencing. These people could not be comforted by kind words or a hug but by social solidarity and the tools for change. Lamentation in the Jewish and Christian traditions has often involved torn clothing and ash but especially ash. The ash reminds us that everything and everyone is eventually reduced to dust. It is a sign of the transience of good fortune and the temporariness of life.

When I lived in Birmingham, we began to experiment with the use of lamentation and ashing at the anniversary of the Iraq occupation. We read out the names of soldiers and civilians killed in Iraq and both marked ourselves with ash and invited those passing by to do the same. Many people joined us; they recognized that this was not a protest but rather a sadness at our shared complicity with a world that leads to such horror and violence. I have used ashing at a nuclear weapons factory and at military bases.

When the elected mayor of Mansfield vetoed the council's decision to fund a local credit union, the churches took to the street in repentance and lamentation. In Mansfield town centre there are six official payday lenders, more than any other kind of business apart from hospitality. In 2013 a group of 40 people from seven churches gathered in our town centre and ashed ourselves for our complicity in the debt economy. We ashed the lintels of the money lenders (seven of them within a two-minute walk of each other), and we sang and prayed as we did so. Doing this both changed us and changed the social situation. Many present became more resolved to work for justice for their neighbours and saw their own responsibility for allowing private debt to spiral out of control. Since then many things have changed, including tighter regulations on money lending, but there is still a long way to go. Lamentation and repentance is simply recognizing our human frailty and temporality in the face of injustice and admitting that we are complicit.

To be enchanted by the earth is to recognize that we are domestic creatures in a constant tussle with the earth for self-rule but in the knowledge that we are most free when we are in partnership with the earth beneath our feet and that it will one day claim us back. In his letter to the Roman Church, the first-century Christian leader, Saint Paul, wrote:

> I consider that the sufferings of this present time are not worth comparing with the glory about to be revealed to us. For the creation waits with eager longing for the revealing of the children of God; for the creation was subjected to futility, not of its own will but by the will of the one who subjected it, in hope that the creation itself will be set free from its bondage to decay and will obtain the freedom of the glory of the children of God. We know that the whole creation has been groaning in labour pains until now; and not only the creation, but we ourselves, who have the first fruits of the Spirit, groan inwardly while we wait for adoption, the redemption of our bodies. (Romans 8.18–23)

He wrote this to a persecuted religious minority at the heart of a ruthless empire. It is a quote from the middle of a long letter to that community, which calls them to radically love both friend and enemy. Yet in the midst of teaching about how to love in the face of political oppression, Paul recognizes humans are not at the centre of the story but that salvation is about all creation, of which humans are a participant.

Between heaven and earth

Resurrection is not unique to the Abrahamic faiths of Judaism, Christianity and Islam. Far from it. Its pedigree goes back to more ancient Near Eastern civilizations and can even be found in the Zen Buddhist tradition as well as in ancient Greek mythology. The Greek god Dionysus bears this mythology in his name which means 'twice born'. Dionysus was torn apart and eaten by Titans on the orders of Zeus's wife, Hera. All that was left of Dionysus was his heart, from which he was remade much as the grapevine is cut right back at the end of its season but regrows again for the following year.

Most stories of resurrection are either stories of the cycles of death and life in nature or the eternal divine rights of rulers. Sometimes they are both together. Stories of resurrection carry us through the winter and spring as we wait for the earth to feed us again. They carry us through seasons of political struggle with the hope of a more just society growing like a seed beneath the snow of injustice. They are stories of life and hope, telling us that neither death nor life are the end, and that neither they nor any powers on earth or above can separate us from the love of God.

Resurrection stories stake out the territory between heaven and earth. They also remind us of the personhood of all nature, or what some people call 'animism'. The word 'anima' is Latin for 'soul'. Animism was originally coined as a pejorative word for indigenous religions that have retained an awareness of the sacredness of all nature in a way that has been eroded in modern Western society. Animism reminds us that all things are 'made to move', a willingness to see the personhood all things and to privilege animation over sentient ability that reintegrates our human being with all other beings. To be re-enchanted by the material world, seeing the spirituality of everyday objects and creatures, is not to say that all things are alive. Rather, all things are a flow of life and death, some are more alive than others, but every branch, bird and mineral somehow occupies the space between heaven and earth where life and death are in a constant dynamic relationship to one another.

To greet the day as we greet a lover is to be re-enchanted with the day and with everything that our senses meet with during it. This animistic approach to life may seem romantic but without romance we cannot hope to act in ways that turn the world as it is into the world as it should be; it helps us access the resources that make that possible. We domesticate the soul as a thing trapped inside the ribcage of *Homo sapiens* when we only look for it inside ourselves. In the end, this is how to re-enchant the activist: to rediscover the sacred oneness of all things and live as though all things have personhood.

This is not to say that all of nature has some universal set of rights of personhood. As nineteenth-century mystic and artist William Blake reminds us, the ox and the lion do not need the same things to thrive, but they do need each other. In recognizing the personhood of all things we see that justice is not a set of laws to be enforced but rather a set of dynamic relationships to be nurtured. If activism is the pursuit of justice, then justice is only known through our commitment to the endless negotiation of our relationship to all things, treating each as a peculiar expression of the whole with personal needs to be met and gifts for the rest. It is a set of dynamic relationships rather than a static blueprint for a perfect society. This book began with the words of the prophet Micah, 'Do justice, love mercy, and walk humbly with your God.' These are three strands of a single cord that is mystical union with all things. Right relationship is justice and wholeness; Jews call it Shalom, Muslims call it Salam and, as we have seen, it is invoked by enchantment.

Billie longed to escape from civilization. He nearly lost his life and lost much of his mental wellbeing in the process. We all carry with us a longing to return to the earth; if we cannot find it through enchantment then we will long to find it in death. This is why the spiritual practice of going barefoot is so profound. Going barefoot allows us to prayerfully listen to the earth from which we came and to which we will return. In doing so we come close enough to death to satisfy our longing and remind ourselves of the wonder of being alive. Barefoot wandering, morbid meditation and spiritual wisdom about death can all humble and revive us so we can be better resourced to do justice. The more we occupy that space between heaven and earth, the more we can be enchanted activists and call others to do the same.

Endnotes

1. McIntosh, A. and Carmichael, M. (2016) *Spiritual Activism: Leadership as Service*. Cambridge: Green Books, pp.63–8.

2. Girard, R. (2001) *I See Satan Fall Like Lightning*. New York: Orbis, p.19.

3. Kayleigh, A. (2015) 'J.K. Rowling, we all know you didn't write Hermione as black in the Harry Potter books – but it doesn't matter.' *Independent*, 21 December. Accessed on 22 May 2016 at www.independent.co.uk/voices/j-k-rowling-we-all-know-you-didnt-write-hermione-as-black-in-the-harry-potter-books-but-it-doesnt-a6781681.html

4. Rowling, J.K. (2015) Twitter. Accessed on 22 May 2016 at https://twitter.com/jk_rowling/status/678888094339366914

5. Penny, L. (2015) 'How to be a genderqueer feminist.' *BuzzFeedNews*, 31 October. Accessed on 22 May 2016 at www.buzzfeed.com/lauriepenny/how-to-be-a-genderqueer-feminist#.kullWeWPK

6. Monroe, J. (2015) 'Please don't call me a girl called Jack. I have something to tell you.' Cooking On a Bootstrap. Accessed on 22 May 2016 at https://cookingonabootstrap.com/2015/10/22/please-dont-call-me-a-girl-called-jack-i-have-something-to-tell-you

7. Easwaran, E. (trans.) (2007) *The Dhammapada*. Berkeley, CA: Nilgiri Press, p.155.

8. Weil, S. (1963) *Gravity and Grace*. London: Routledge, p.33.

9. Weil, S. (1963) *Gravity and Grace*. London: Routledge, p.103.

10. Weil, S. (1963) *Gravity and Grace*. London: Routledge, p.47.

11. Weil, S. (1963) *Gravity and Grace*. London: Routledge, p.78.

12. Parker, A. (2013) *The Bible as Politics: The Rape of Dinah and Other Stories*. Winchester: Christian Alternative, p.7.

13. Buy Nothing Christmas (n.d.) 'Resources.' Accessed on 22 May 2016 at http://buynothingchristmas.org/resources/carols.html

14. Soelle, D. (2001) *The Silent Cry: Mysticism and Resistance*. Minneapolis, MN: Fortress Press, p.35.

15. Priests for Equality (2007) *The Inclusive Bible*. Plymouth: Rowman and Littlefield.

16. Theos (2013) 'The Spirit of Things Unseen: belief in post-religious Britain.' Accessed on 22 May 2016 at www.theosthinktank.co.uk/publications/2013/10/17/the-spirit-of-things-unseen-belief-in-post-religious-britain

17. Cavanaugh, W.T. (1995) 'A fire strong enough to consume the house: The wars of religion and the rise of the state.' *Modern Theology* 11.4, p.398.

18. Inclusive Church (2004–2016) Accessed on 5 July 2016 at http://inclusive-church.org.uk

19. endhungerfast.co.uk

20. Tejvan Pettinger (2016) 'UK National Debt.' *Economics Help*. Accessed on 6 July 2016 at www.economicshelp.org/blog/334/uk-economy/uk-national-debt

21. Beattie, J. (2014) '27 bishops slam David Cameron's welfare reforms as creating a national crisis in unprecedented attack.' *Mirror*, 19 February. Accessed on 13 June 2016 at www.mirror.co.uk/news/uk-news/27-bishops-slam-david-camerons-3164033

22. Cross, S. (2014, 9 March) 'True Fasting?' [weblog post]. Accessed on 22 May 2016 at https://simoncross.wordpress.com/2014/03/09/true-fasting

23. Gandhi, M.K. (2001) *An Autobiograpy: Or The Story of My Experiments with Truth* (trans. Mahadev Desai). London: Penguin, p.313.

24. Monbiot, G. (2013) *Feral: Searching for Enchantment on the Frontiers of Rewilding*. London: Allen Lane, p.60.

25. Monbiot, G. (2013) *Feral: Searching for Enchantment on the Frontiers of Rewilding*. London: Allen Lane, p.46.